The Short Story
in America
1900-1950

The Short Story in America

1900-1950

Ray B. West, Jr.

University of Iowa

Essay Index Reprint Series

BOOKS FOR LIBRARIES
A Division of Arno Press, Inc.
New York • 1979

54482

INTERNATIONAL STANDARD BOOK NUMBER:

0-8369-0982-8

LIBRARY OF CONGRESS CATALOG CARD NUMBER:

68-55863

PRINTED IN THE UNITED STATES OF AMERICA

To write a series of good little tales
I deem ample work for a lifetime.
—HENRY JAMES

PREFACE

I SUPPOSE *no one knows exactly how many short stories are written in America in a single day—a single month—a single year. The knowledge would be as unimpressive as statistics concerning any other type of birth. What is important is not the knowledge that every hour of the year, somewhere in America, an author puts the finishing touches to his manuscript, inserts it in an envelope, and mails it hopefully to a publisher. The important fact is seldom recognized when it occurs. The birth of a masterpiece—like the birth of a future president—is singularly lacking in those qualities which will later come to make it seem so important an occasion.*

Yet the birth of a work of art differs from the birth of a child in one important respect: it comes into the world full-blown and mature. Its obscurity is not the result of any quality—or the absence of any quality—which it, itself, possesses or as yet fails to possess. It does not, of itself, make its way in the world. It lies inert, passive, awaiting the recognition which is its due. When recognition fails, it fails because of the stupidity and insensibility which surrounds the work in life. When recognition comes, it comes because someone, somewhere—the common or uncommon reader, the anthologist, the professor of literature, the professional critic, or, what is more likely, all of them together—has discovered those qualities which make it great. The appearance of a book such as this one represents merely the formal acknowledgment.

In its most important aspect this sort of book is not the result of its author alone. It must acknowledge the collaboration—the genius, the taste, and the judgment—of many others: the imagination which produced a work of art in the first place, the editorial mind which first gave it recognition, the discriminating readers who read and enjoyed it. The critic depends upon these collaborators for his subject. He goes beyond them only in degree, but it is a degree which often leads to dizzying heights. He tells—or attempts to tell—the author why he wrote as he did, the publisher why he published, and the reader why he read with enjoyment. In short, he recognizes the what, *and he attempts to explain the* why.

Such a claim may seem pretentious—and it is. It becomes insufferable, however, only when the critic pretends to infallible judgment, either as a result of his own genius and knowledge or as a result of the system which he practices. My own view is that critics are notoriously fallible. But I distinguish between critics and criticism. Criticism is less fallible. Critics write books; criticism produces judgments. Criticism is the sum of all that critics have written—the sum total of history, biography, scholarship, and aesthetic knowledge. Its evaluations are as final as is anything fashioned by the hand of man. However, in the degree that it succeeds in its ultimate aim, it becomes correspondingly less human.

I find it necessary to say this in the Preface to so short and unpretentious a book as The Short Story in America, 1900–1950 *because there has recently been an increasing tendency to read books by critics as though they were books of criticism. There may even have been a tendency to write books with this attitude. I wish to discourage such reading and to disclaim such intentions, not because I make no claims and pretend to no judgments, but because in writing this book I have been more than usually aware of exceptional limitations both in myself and in my subject. I can speak only of the latter. First of all, the short story as a form is so new that few general studies—few definitions— exist. Second, the relationship between the short story and other literary forms—particularly the novel, to which it is so closely related—has never been adequately pointed out. Third, the time span covered by this book, while it represents an important and exciting period in the development of the short story, is still too close to us to allow the most satisfactory over-all perspective; our view of the past fifty years is still obscured by unresolved controversy and conflicting attitudes.*

Still, there must be a time to start, and any time would probably seem either too early or too late. Perspective does not come from distance alone but is perceived through the relationship of objects on the literary landscape. I can only hope that this book may serve as one of those objects, a landmark, a point of orientation for those readers who may have found themselves agreeably across the border but have not yet lost the sense of being in a foreign land.

I am indebted to E. F. McGuire, Managing Editor of The Western Review, *State University of Iowa, who compiled the Bibliography appended to this volume.*

RAY B. WEST, JR.

CONTENTS

The Short Story
in America

THE AMERICAN SHORT STORY
AT MID-CENTURY

HE history of the short story as a literary
form is brief. It is the only form developed recently enough
so that the American writer could participate in its development from the beginning. While there have been examples
of short fiction in the history of literature almost since the
beginning of recorded time, we have come recently to see
that there is more to the short story than the mere facts of
its brevity and its being written in prose. The earliest prose
narratives of which we have record are probably a collection
of tales, dating from approximately 4000 B.C., entitled *Tales
of the Magicians*. Other such collections have come from
the Hindus, the Hebrews, the Greeks, and the Arabs. The
Middle Ages and the Renaissance supplied us with beast
fables, picaresque tales, and romances. But the conception
of the individual short tale as a work of art, comparable to

lyric or dramatic verse, even to the novel, is of comparatively recent origin. No final definition of the short story has ever been achieved. Indeed, it would probably be true to say that we shall never arrive at an adequate definition. It may even be true to maintain, as many do, that to define the short story would be to impose limitations upon it that would destroy much of its attraction for us. Nevertheless, there is something in the nature of man which leads him to generalize, to organize, and to account for his behavior. Such is the impulse which leads to definition.

Historically, the earliest forms of stories, such as the *gesta*, were tales of action—adventure (the word is from the same root as are our English words, "jest" and "gesture"). The Italian and German terms are *novella* and *novellen*, which, like *gesta*, are usually used in the plural to suggest a collection. They suggest our English word "news"—things new or novel. The English word "tale" (as the French, *conte*) suggests a telling—something told or recounted. The modern word "story" has its roots in both the Old French, *estoire* and the Latin, *historia*—history. Thus we accommodate ourselves to the relatively modern view of prose narrative as essentially a retelling of something which actually happened, whether pretended or actual; that is, history in the sense that both *A Journal of the Plague Year* and *Moll Flanders* are histories.

Strangely enough, the first American to write outstanding short narratives in prose used none of these terms. Trained first as an artist, Washington Irving saw his own early tales as pictorial representations of places and events and thus called them "sketches." Such a word was current in Germany, where J. L. Tieck, for instance, called his first collection of short tales *Die Gemälde* (pictures). There may be some justification for considering the sketch a separate form, as some writers do, differentiating it from the tale by pointing to its emphasis upon atmosphere and scene, its subordination of action and adventure. If so, it is a form which as yet lacks anything like full development, or—as is more likely—it is a romantic means of catching the atmosphere of remote places. It would seem more reasonable to say that both the sketch and the tale (if there ever was a real distinction) have been absorbed into our modern concept of the short story.

Certainly the three Americans whose accomplishments in the writing of the short prose narrative were of most importance to us drew from all sources without concern for type or genre. Nathaniel Hawthorne, Edgar Allan Poe, and Herman Melville all called their productions "tales"—as did Irving a later volume (*Tales of a Traveller*, 1824). Hawthorne's first published collection of stories was called *Twice-Told Tales*. Poe's was called *Tales of the Grotesque and Arabesque*. Melville called his early collection *The Piazza Tales*. One of the earliest—if not the earliest—uses of the term "story" in the title of a work in English was by Henry James in *Daisy Miller: A Study; And Other Stories*, published in 1883. The word "story" has been used almost exclusively since the beginning of the present century.

The name of a form does not, of course, tell us all that we need know in arriving at a usable definition. There is little evidence that anyone has been particularly concerned with defining the limits of a tale, or in distinguishing between a tale and a sketch, or a tale and an essay, before the middle of the nineteenth century; and strangely enough, in America, it was the publication of a single-volume edition *Twice-Told Tales* in 1851 which gave rise to the first serious attempts to define the nature of the tale or story. Edgar Allan Poe had already extended his review of Hawthorne's collection of tales into a critical definition which has had a good deal of influence, both good and bad, over the century since it first appeared. Hawthorne followed with a less concise statement than Poe's in the Preface to his second edition of the tales—less a definition than an explanation of what he had attempted to accomplish. Though Hawthorne's Preface was written after Poe's article, perhaps even as a reply to it, we might begin by examining it, for it is a much quieter and less assertive document than Poe's, a negative rather than a positive statement. Its tone is gently ironic, so that we must be careful about taking the words too literally. In general, Hawthorne says, the stories contain too little passion and too much sentiment; instead of scenes and characters from actual life, they present symbolic figures and allegoric situations. In part he replies to his own charges by suggesting that "they have none of the abstruseness of idea, or obscurity of expression, which mark the written communications of a solitary mind with itself." (Poe had charged that some of his stories were essays rather than tales.) Hawthorne goes on to say that "they never need translation. . . . [They are written in] the style of a man of society. . . . [They are] attempts . . . to open an intercourse with the world." Hawthorne seems here to suggest that the tales have an objective existence apart from the author, an impersonality; they exist, not as the meditations of a solitary mind, but as objects capable of projecting themselves into the outside world; they do not need translation through the mind of the author. Here is a view which is to be re-emphasized later by so important a figure as Henry James.

Perhaps the most significant thing about Poe's review— aside from his serious and sympathetic reading of Hawthorne—is his emphatic statement that such tales "belong to the highest region of Art—an Art subservient to genius of a very lofty order." The definition itself is almost too well known to require repeating, but since it has had a singular effect upon the craft of short-story writing, particularly in America, and since it is brief, let us take another look at it:

A skilful literary artist has construed a tale. If wise, he has not fashioned his thoughts to accommodate his incidents; but having conceived, with deliberate care, a certain unique or single *effect* to be wrought out, he then invents such incidents—he then combines such events as may best aid him in establishing this preconceived effect. If his very initial sentence tend not to the outbringing of this effect, then he has failed in his first step. In the whole composition there should be no word written, of which the tendency, direct or indirect, is not to the one pre-established design.

If we are offended somewhat by the simplicity and the too absolute tone of this pronouncement, we must nevertheless grant the general rightness of it. Poe was among the first, if not actually the first, to conceive of the short story as belonging to the highest region of art and to suggest the formal discipline necessary to achieving it. Perhaps the greatest weakness of his definition is the implication that the creation of a story is a highly conscious, almost mechanical, process. On one level, it is, of course, and it may be that in framing his statement Poe was unconsciously rebelling against the nineteenth century's excessive faith in the private sensibility and inspiration of the artist and the accidental nature of art. In another article ("The Philosophy of Composition") he went much further in his account of his own procedure in writing "The Raven," but few of us today concede that this account is even an accurate description of Poe's own creative procedure.

Herman Melville seems to have made no clear distinction between the short story and the novel. He wrote short stories

—and very good ones, as we have come recently to see. For the most part, however, their length was dictated by the fact that he was writing for magazine publication. In tone and method they owe a good deal to Hawthorne's example. Important to us is the fact that Melville's attitude toward his craft, particularly during the period when he composed his short stories, became more and more uncompromising. Especially significant is a statement which he made in his Preface to a volume of verse: "It is not the purpose of literature to purvey news. For news consult the *Almanac de Gotha.*"

If the critical revaluations of our own day have tended to exalt Melville and Hawthorne and to reduce the stature of Edgar Allan Poe, it is nevertheless to these three men that we must look for the beginnings of the short story in America—the short story as we know it today. I do not mean that the American story was an isolated and independent phenomenon. Much could be written about the influence, direct or indirect, of such European writers as Goethe and Tieck in Germany; Pushkin, Gogol, and Chekhov in Russia; Mérimée, Gautier, Maupassant, Flaubert, Daudet, and Zola in France; Scott, Hardy, Conrad, and Kipling in England. Also, we should bear in mind the progress of the romantic movement across Europe in the eighteenth and nineteenth centuries, noting its effect not only upon ideas and institutions but upon literary forms as well. It has even been suggested that the status of international copyright (which made the pirating of novels by foreign authors more profitable in America than the legitimate publication of native authors) had much to do with the growth of the short story in our country. Yet there were factors typically American or the product of American genius, which has had much to do with the development of the short-story form. There was, for instance, the development of periodicals and magazines in America with a consequent demand for work which could be presented, whole and complete, within a single issue. There was a body of native materials which, combined with more or less typical nineteenth-century American attitudes, determined the method or technique by which such materials could be shaped into a suitable form. There was, finally, the universal desire to perfect both technique and form to the highest possible degree—an urge no more typically American than it is typically Athenian, no more a characteristic of the year A.D. 1900 than of the year B.C. 300. Yet the history of the American short story during its brief existence is the tracing of the creative talent, even occasionally the genius, of American authors in their struggle to subdue the intractable material of life through the media of art and talent.

ii

The most common means of ordering the history of any art form is to arrange it in chronological periods. Since our subject is the development of the American short story since 1900, we must assume that one can distinguish, somehow, between the work done in one period and another. If this is true, and if the ordering is done by centuries, we must attempt to get at the differences represented between one century and another. Clearly, this difference will seldom represent a total shift of viewpoint, but only a shift in what we might call the "specific gravity" of one age contrasted with another. With the perspective of time, for instance, we can conceive of a dominantly neoclassic eighteenth century in England opposed to a dominantly romantic nineteenth century. Yet, such a view demands the perspective of time, and time is too short in the case of our present subject to allow anything except the vaguest kind of vision. Poe, Hawthorne, and Melville belong clearly to the nineteenth century so far as their writing careers are concerned. Poe died in 1849, at an early age; Hawthorne lived until 1864; Melville died in 1891. Also, we must not forget that there is a way of looking at literature which makes any great writer more contemporary than a host of minor writers of our own day. What about such writers as William Dean Howells, Mark Twain, and Bret Harte? What about Stephen Crane and Henry James? Clearly our chronological ordering must depend a good deal upon some ideological center of gravity, for Stephen Crane, who did all of his writing before 1900, seems in many respects more closely related to the early years of the twentieth century than do Mark Twain, who died in 1910, or Henry James, who did not die until 1916. Perhaps we can come nearer to a reasonable chronological ordering if we neglect the date 1900 altogether and, while retaining the chronological ordering, group our authors about the significant historical dates of the period—the three great wars. We might, then, propose the following for the first three periods:

Pre-Civil War (1830–1860)

Edgar Allan Poe, Nathaniel Hawthorne, Herman Melville.

Post-Civil War (1860–1890)

William Dean Howells, Mark Twain, Bret Harte, Ambrose Bierce.

Pre-World War I (1890–1915)

Stephen Crane, Hamlin Garland, Henry James, Edith Wharton, Jack London, O. Henry.

Many difficulties of such an ordering are obvious. We have, for instance, little reason for including Ambrose

Bierce in the second category; we shall find difficulty in reconciling the inclusion of Henry James, O. Henry, and Hamlin Garland—strange bedfellows—within the third. Nevertheless, granting this difficulty, let us use such a method for the remainder of our present century:

Post-World War I (1915–1930)

Ring Lardner, Dorothy Canfield Fisher, Theodore Dreiser, Sherwood Anderson, F. Scott Fitzgerald, Ellen Glasgow, Ernest Hemingway, Wilbur Daniel Steele, Sinclair Lewis, Conrad Aiken, Gertrude Stein, Glenway Wescott, William Faulkner, William Carlos Williams.

Pre-World War II (1930–1940)

Erskine Caldwell, James Thurber, William Saroyan, John Steinbeck, James T. Farrell, Katherine Anne Porter, Kay Boyle, Caroline Gordon, J. P. Marquand, Thomas Wolfe, Robert Penn Warren.

Post-World War II (1940–1950)

Eudora Welty, Walter Van Tilburg Clark, Irwin Shaw, Peter Taylor, Wallace Stegner, J. F. Powers, Mark Schorer, Delmore Schwartz, Carson McCullers, Truman Capote.

The inclusion of so many names in the last three categories does not necessarily mean that the twentieth century has been in this proportion more successful than the preceding century. In fact, even the inclusion of a group of writers so young as those in the final group must be considered an act of speculation more than of critical judgment. In any case, it seems obvious that such ordering by chronological periods can be of but limited value. It is true that there is at times a very definite relationship between an art form and the milieu in which it is written, but the present scene

is still cluttered by minor events, ideas, and personal loyal-
ties which time will eventually clear away, and perhaps our
first responsibility is to penetrate this fog, if we can, and see
clearly the sharp landscape below.

Aside from the perceptive comments which Edgar Allan
Poe made in his attempted definition of the short story,
he made others which seem now to have created confusion
rather than order. He attempted, for instance, to divide the
story into two types—those which he called tales of ratiocina-
tion and those he termed tales of atmosphere or effect. What
Poe meant by this division we can understand best by re-
calling his own stories. The first type is characterized by
the ingeniously plotted story—as "The Gold Bug" or "The
Purloined Letter"—where the effect is made primarily as the
result of an interest aroused by a close following of the details of complicated action and a final comprehension of its
infallible logic. The second depended less upon action than
it did upon the multiplication of atmospheric details, as in
"The Fall of the House of Usher." Now there is nothing essentially wrong with an attempt to define an art form according to type, as Poe did here. But a type is not the artificial
imposition of a definition. A true type must grow out of the
conditions of the material in which the artist works, or out
of his own temperament, or—what is more likely—out of
both. Poe's concept of the ratiocinative tale developed into
the more or less empty form of the detective story or the ingeniously plotted stories of our popular magazines. At its
best, it produced an O. Henry, at its second best, a Jack London. The atmospheric tale, in the sense that it came to be
known as such, produced little more than Poe's own tales of
horror, most of which seem to us now to be forced and sentimental, and perhaps the same applies to the so-called "local-
color" stories of a writer like Bret Harte, who seems to have

falsely exploited atmospheric effects at the expense of psychological and moral truth.

The real fact now would seem to be that Poe was more concerned with the preconceived (or artificially conceived) structure than he was with grounding his art in the life around him. His was a dilettante's interest, focused more on the mechanics of form than on form as an expression, an embodiment, of human experience. By contrast, Nathaniel Hawthorne, who at first glance appears even more remote than Poe, is seen now as having the principal concerns of his time and ours centrally located in his work. We have come to see that this remoteness was one not of subject matter but of technique. He might write a story about a love affair between the exotic daughter of an Italian sorcerer and her student lover, set in a remote place and time and embracing events which our common sense tells us are clearly impossible; yet, the underlying theme is so embodied in the tale and is so much a part of our own human experience that we find it not only moving but comprehensively, wholly satisfying.

I do not mean to suggest that a story, in order to be thus satisfactory, needs the remoteness of locale and of manners which Hawthorne and many writers of Hawthorne's time seemed to prefer. Melville and Henry James could write movingly of contemporary figures and events, as they often did, while nothing seems more contemporary than certain stories by Stephen Crane, Ernest Hemingway, or William Faulkner. Yet, there is a kind of distinction which we might make—perhaps *must* make—a distinction which comes very close to defining the age as much as it does the short stories which our age has produced. Hawthorne, for instance, was less interested in the surface reality of his tales than he was in the underlying themes—what he called "the truths of the human heart" and what we, no doubt, would consider the psychological implications of his subject: the substructure of symbol and myth. A writer such as Howells or Stephen Crane—or to find more extreme examples, such as Hamlin Garland or Theodore Dreiser—would be more interested in the fidelity with which they reproduced the surface features of the life about them. I know of no satisfactory name by which to designate the first kind of story. The term "symbolic" is too confining, and as a word it has taken on a coloring which many modern readers find distasteful. The second type we may, for the sake of momentary convenience, call the "naturalistic" story, both as stemming from a loosely defined movement known as literary naturalism and as focusing its attention upon that part of man's experience in which he is most closely allied to nature.

Such definition has the advantage of suggesting dominant attitudes and states of mind; thus are generalizations not artificially imposed upon an author. However, we must remember that merely to name a writer a *symbolist*, a *realist*, or a *naturalist* is not to say all that there is to say about him or his work. It is an aid to memory—a starting point—perhaps merely the most convenient point from which to begin. We can say, for instance, that literary naturalism describes a particular manner of viewing life, that since life is the source of art, whatever views the artist holds will be reflected in his work. We shall then need to go a step further and ask: "What is the source of those ideas?" When we have sought and found that source, perhaps we shall have found an adequate and satisfactory basis upon which to order our knowledge of the short stories of our immediate past.

William Dean Howells may have been impressed by the concepts formulated by Emile Zola, founder of a more or less doctrinaire movement which came out of France late in the nineteenth century, but Howells's attraction to Zola's theories was not wholly the result of indoctrinization. More likely, Zola formulated for Howells a possible response to many of the problems which became clearly visible in America in the period following the Civil War: the difficulties of reconstruction in the South, the rapid rise of industrialism in the North, the vigorous expansion of the frontier to the West. Add to this the equalitarian ideas of traditional American republicanism and the interests of a nation in which the greater part of its geographic area was still composed of natural wilderness, and it is not difficult to understand the appeal of a philosophy which saw all men as equals, not only before God, but in nature—a philosophy which saw literature as a means by which inequality and injustice might be exposed, social democratic ideals of freedom and security achieved. To do justice to such a concept would perhaps demand a separate study. Briefly, however, it might be said that literary naturalism made less of an impression upon the history of the short story than it did upon the history of the American novel. In the first place, the short story because of its length demanded a greater preoccupation with literary techniques than the naturalist, who was in an important sense antiliterary, was willing or able to grant. In the second place, the concept itself when carried to its logical extreme exposed itself as being in opposition to ideas embodied in traditional great works which the writer—who was an artist as well as a thinker—was unwilling or unable to discard.

On a less abstract level, however, some of the ideas inherent in literary naturalism did contribute toward the shaping of the American short story into something unique, more the outgrowth of its own background than the product of European thought and example. Chief among these is the habit of language (the voice—the style) which developed, perhaps first of all as the result of the American colonists' experience in fashioning a civilization in the face of an amazing but recalcitrant nature. Of almost equal importance, however, were the attitudes toward nature which the colonists brought with them from Europe, the concepts of natural goodness and natural rights, an interest and faith in primitive virtue—all part of his rebellion against aristocratic ideas and what had come to seem the artificial nature of the social structure of Europe. Thus, the early hero of our folk literature was the rootless but shrewd Yankee pedlar who traveled the trails and highways of the seaboard colonies, living by his wits and outwitting the more pretentious and settled of his countrymen. Later the pedlar became the frontiersman, still a man rootless and wandering, but one living close to the marvels of nature, reporting his own prowess and the prowess of nature as though they were one and the same thing, reporting them with the impassivity of nature, a pretended ineloquence which became the broadest kind of irony. This is the mask—the voice—through which the American has come to speak, his characteristic tone. It is the voice of Ralph Waldo Emerson (that shrewd Yankee) as well as of Artemus Ward (the wild humorist of the mountains). Beneath the innocent, matter-of-fact reportorial voice of the frontier humorist ran a deeper current of social comment. What could Harvard College supply to prepare a young man for his entrance into the wilderness of the West—even the wilderness of American politics? What knowledge brought from Europe could compete with native shrewdness in dealing with wild animals, Sioux Indians, and the greed of those seeking political preferment or California's gold? The masked voice became the trade-mark of the pedlar, the frontiersman, and even of a certain kind of politician—the hero of American mythology. At his best he became an Ishmael, a Huckleberry Finn, or a Christopher Newman; at his most common, the pathetic flotsam of Bret Harte's romantic tales. A whaling ship, a frontier river community, or the gold fields of the West were his Harvard College. Confronted by Europe, as were Twain's "innocents abroad," he saw through the subterfuge and sham of the Old World's civilization.

On this level, however, it was all too simple and too innocent, as even Mark Twain came to recognize. Hawthorne and Melville had seen the evil lurking beneath the innocent appearance of the natural world. The journey of the American innocent into the world was not a success story (as it had seemed at first to Twain), so much as it was the subject for tragedy—the good man's recognition of his limitations, his fate; and this knowledge Europe, despite its complacent decadence, could give. It was no accident that so many of Henry James's heroes and heroines were Americans. And they did not derive merely from the fact that James was an American. The American myth was naturalistic in the sense that it put such value upon those characteristics of innocence and primitivism which derive from Rousseau's view of the natural world. As such it shared the antiliterary, antihumanistic views of the literary naturalism derived from Zola. Literary naturalism in its extreme social emphasis could see art as a weapon for social good, but the aesthetic assumptions of Hawthorne, Melville, and even Twain contained the contradictions inherited from the concepts of their time (the nineteenth century) and place (an expanding American nation), without the means of accommodating such concepts to an increasing awareness of the humanistic importance of their art and the existence of truth outside the bounds of the American myth. Henry James was the first significant American author to see clearly that the importance of the mythological concept of innocent, natural man consisted in his usefulness as a tragic figure in the highest sense, not as a mere illustration of national virtue.

Realizing this, it is not too difficult to account for the relative neglect of James during the last years of his career and the first years following his death. This accounts, too, for a similar neglect of Hawthorne and Melville and a failure to recognize the true value of Mark Twain, for all of these authors came finally to recognize intuitively what James saw more clearly—that the American story was a story of initiation, a recognition of the significance of evil, a pessimistic rather than an optimistic view of man. The years between the close of the Civil War and the end of World War I were essentially years of optimism in America. Except for the South, burdened by problems of reconstruction and producing few writers, America seemed destined to fulfill the prophecies of the nineteenth century. Such writings as the novels of Howells and Stephen Crane, Hamlin Garland's tales of the settling of the prairies, Frank Norris's novels of California farmers and Chicago businessmen were all dreary enough in tone and subject matter but filled with the optimism of social progress. It is difficult to recall now that in the years preceding World War I and during a brief flurry of revived social interest in the depression years of the 1930's such works seemed to represent the mainstream of American fiction. Hawthorne and Melville were puzzles to us. Twain was cherished for his humor alone. James was dismissed as pretty but insignificant. During and following the war, however, a generation of writers appeared to challenge such a view, to challenge it both in theory and in a practical evaluation of the works themselves.

It seems important to say that such revision of attitude stemmed from two obvious sources: 1. from academic critics

who, under various designations or schools, arose to call attention to traditional literary and social values; 2. from a
group of young Southerners who discovered in the historical
background of their region evidence of moral and social values threatened by the concepts of naturalism and social progressivism. There were also underlying social causes, such
as the final closing of the frontier and the disillusion produced by the end of the war and the obvious loss of the peace.
This was the period of the so-called "lost generation," which
we have come lately to see not so much as a generation
floundering amidst the wreck of its lost cause as a generation on the one hand almost belligerently seeking new values, on the other, consciously re-examining old ones. It has
come to seem only reasonable that such a period should re-
discover and revalue the concerns of Hawthorne, Melville,
and James.

What were those concerns? Briefly, we might say that they
were the relationship between literature and life—literature
as a means of viewing life. While naturalism saw art as a
means of controlling social action, the more traditional view
would see it as an examination of the various views and attitudes toward life. Where the naturalist would accept only
a materialistic view of life and decry all else as myth, the
traditional view would see myth as a reflection of a richer
and more ambiguous reality. Naturalism would see life as
single and decry evil merely as the absence of good; the traditionalist would see life as multiple, with evil as a positive
force contesting good and complicating man's problem of
moral choice.

The relationship between these ideas and a literary form
such as the short story is, I hope, by now obvious. The traditionalist is he who values the technique of his art because it
is a means whereby the richness and complexity of life may

be known and felt. The naturalist tends to emphasize the materials—the subject matter—of his craft. In extreme cases, he even may come to feel that the techniques of art distort and violate the reality which he sees in nature. Having said as much, however, one should be careful to note that such extremes rarely occur. In the finest of our writing, whether the writer is committed to a naturalistic view (as Stephen Crane was, for instance) or to more traditional views (as was Henry James), the result has been a firmer grounding of the short story in the materials of life—what we commonly speak of as reality—with no actual disrespect for traditional techniques. The difference, in literature at least, is a difference of degree, not of kind.

iii

With a view of art, then, which sees literature—including the short story—as a means of dealing with the total world of reality, we return again to the problem of definition. Here we must take note of the accumulation in the first half of our century of a body of literary criticism in America which I believe to have profoundly affected the modern short story. Our purpose is not to trace the development of this critical movement, except briefly, to indicate its relationship to the writing of the short story. Insofar as this criticism deals with fiction, it undoubtedly stems primarily from the writing of Henry James, not only from his critical writings, but from the example of his novels and stories as well. James, like Poe, saw fiction as one of the highest forms of art, perhaps the form most characteristic of our age. He liked to think of himself, however, as a realist; and by that he meant not what we have considered the primary qualities of the naturalists, but only that art should be firmly based on life. Art was for

him an autonomous form of knowledge, as science or philosophy is autonomous. The structure of fiction was organic,
the truths which it revealed were implicit rather than explicit, and its appeal was to be made not to the intellect alone
—or even primarily—but to the intellect in conjunction with
the emotions. As such, its effect was similar to the effect one
gets from a real-life situation but refined and concentrated
beyond the wasteful and untidy responses one makes in life.
The means by which such effects are realized we learn by
studying James's works in conjunction with his remarkable
notebooks and his Prefaces (originally written for the New
York edition of his works, since edited and published by R.
P. Blackmur under the title *The Art of the Novel*). We can
read also James's studies of other writers in *Partial Portraits,*
as well as his general article on "The Art of Fiction." We can
study an examination of James's method in Percy Lubbock's
The Craft of Fiction, and we can see his attitudes applied
critically in such articles as Allen Tate's "Techniques of Fiction" and Mark Schorer's "Technique as Discovery."

Yet James proposed nothing that either Hawthorne or
Melville had not achieved in their best work, nor can we believe that his critical writing made any deep impression over
the years immediately preceding and following his death.
Rather, it was James's example and the impression his work
made upon writers of talent several years following his death
that are of first importance. There is little doubt that it was
James's prose which inspired Ford Madox Ford to make the
remark (later given circulation by Ezra Pound) that poetry
of our day should be at least as well written as prose. It seems
clear, too, that James's work was as much as anything the
result of his attitude toward his craft; and it is this attitude,
reflected in the work itself, to which we refer primarily when
we speak of James's influence upon the present.

The history of this interest in Henry James and in the problems which that interest represents might be suggested as follows: 1. the early enthusiasm of Ezra Pound for the writings of James, an enthusiasm which he no doubt first received from Ford Madox Ford; 2. the publication of Percy Lubbock's *The Craft of Fiction* in 1921, a book which has at its core James's concept of the central intelligence as a unifying and dramatic technique; 3. the appearance of the James issue of *Hound & Horn* in 1934, which many have seen as the beginning of the present interest in James; 4. the publication in 1943 of *Understanding Fiction* by Cleanth Brooks and Robert Penn Warren, a college textbook which, like their earlier *Understanding Poetry,* had a revolutionary effect upon the manner in which such literature was taught in the university. By 1950 most of the so-called "New Critics" had written upon fiction, had in fact seemed to be shifting the center of their interest from poetry to fiction: Brooks, Warren, Tate, John Crowe Ransom, Blackmur, and Mark Schorer. In 1949 and 1950 four additional textbooks of the short story appeared, all based more or less upon James's concept of fiction as a significant art form and concerned with the problem of isolating and examining the formal aspects of the short story.[1]

Such modern criticism, taking its lead from James, sees the short story as an organic whole in which none of the parts may be considered in isolation, in which each element must contribute its full share toward the achieving of a final effect. Incident must not exist for its own sake, as it seemed so frequently to do in the stories of O. Henry or in the superficial

[1] Ray B. West, Jr. and Robert Wooster Stallman, *The Art of Modern Fiction* (New York, Rinehart, 1949); Caroline Gordon and Allen Tate, *The House of Fiction* (New York, Scribner, 1950); Mark Schorer, *The Story: A Critical Anthology* (New York, Prentice-Hall, 1950); *Modern Short Stories: A Critical Anthology,* ed. Robert B. Heilman (New York, Harcourt, 1950).

fiction of the popular magazines. Action must grow out of the conflicting motives of the characters. Likewise, atmosphere should not represent a merely sentimental coloring of scene, as it did in the so-called local-color stories of the turn of the century. Atmosphere becomes one of the techniques whereby the total scene achieves its appropriate tone as the result of an underlying consistency of attitude toward the subject. Theme, or idea, represents not the mere drawing of a moral—the reducing of the story to a fable or a merely illustrative statement. The idea must be embodied by the structure itself, must become as much an integrated segment of the total work as are the characters and the action. Thus, finally, in such a view, it is impossible for the critic to concern himself with the action of a story without considering what such action signifies, what characters are concerned and how, whether their acts are fully motivated and according to what moral concepts, and whether the whole emanates its appropriate tonal quality.

Yet, the line of development from Henry James to the present was not as straight as we have made it seem. The influence of Flaubert in France, Chekhov in Russia, and James Joyce in Ireland must also be taken into account, as must the importance of the newer psychological theories. The writing of the New Critics has affected our attitude toward the short story as a form, but if we except our most recent generation of short-story writers, of whom it is too early to speak with real certainty, we must admit that modern criticism has had only an indirect effect upon the major writers themselves. It can be shown, I believe, that Ernest Hemingway has been seriously and conscientiously concerned with the problems of his craft. It has been customary to attribute this concern to the tutelage of Gertrude Stein, whom Hemingway knew in Paris following World

War I, and it is known that Hemingway is not without an appreciation of the example of Ezra Pound (of whom he said recently: "He spawned a whole generation of poets") and of James Joyce, to whom he inscribed and sent copies of his early work. Hemingway says that he learned his craft from Maupassant, Dumas, Daudet, Stendhal, Flaubert, Baudelaire, and Rimbaud, at least half of whom were the masters of Henry James. Both Hemingway and William Faulkner were introduced to French literature through Sherwood Anderson, who had met Gertrude Stein in Paris as early as 1921. Anderson had met Hemingway in Chicago, and he was in Paris when Hemingway returned to Europe. The year following his visit to Europe, Anderson became acquainted with William Faulkner in New Orleans, and the six months they spent together is commonly thought to represent the most significant period in William Faulkner's literary apprenticeship.

Despite the fact that I believe this increased awareness of the problems of craftsmanship on the part of the American short-story writer to be crucial in an understanding of what has happened to the writing of fiction in our century, I do not wish to make too much of it. There remains the matter of the talent of the individual writer. Individual talent must never be forgotten, but it is a subject with which the critic and the historian can have little to do. We may speculate and say that writers such as Mark Twain and Thomas Wolfe, whose native talent has never been denied, wasted time and energy by an incomplete understanding of the problems of their craft. Contrariwise, we may speculate that so conscious a craftsman as Katherine Anne Porter, by the very fact of her awareness, placed a restraint upon her talent which has limited her output and confined her scope. Yet even so, such speculation does not wholly explain the supreme achievement represented by Twain's *Huckleberry Finn*—one of the great works of fiction of our time; nor does it adequately account for the great number of outstanding works produced by Henry James. Perhaps we are on safer ground when we assume that the short story, since it represents a limited length and scope, does demand a certain conscious awareness. In any case, we can point to the fact that those authors who have excelled in the American short story have all indicated a deliberate awareness of the problems of their craft: Nathaniel Hawthorne, Herman Melville, Henry James, Ernest Hemingway, and William Faulkner; those who have not had this awareness—Mark Twain, Theodore Dreiser, and Thomas Wolfe—are best known for their longer fiction.

I think there is no doubt that we can say that the twentieth century in America has seen the short story mature as a form of literature as genuinely artful as such older forms as lyric or narrative verse, more popular than drama. To say as much does not detract from the perception of those nineteenth-century authors, from Poe to Henry James, whose genuine concern for the problems of their craft represents the inheritance of our age. It means only that in the twentieth century there is a more widespread recognition of the validity of their judgments. It is undoubtedly too early to make any very definite evaluation of the over-all accomplishments of our own age. The most we can do is to continue, as our predecessors have done, to seek the basis upon which such a judgment shall finally rest.

I have indicated my belief that at least two authors, whose careers fall wholly within the present half century, Ernest Hemingway and William Faulkner, have accomplishments sufficient to allow their ranking alongside the three great masters of the last century, accomplishments which rest not only upon the achievement of one or two unusually significant stories but upon the creation of a body of short fiction matched in America only by that of Henry James. As with the past century, where the work of such authors as Edgar Allan Poe and Stephen Crane was overshadowed only by the works of Hawthorne, Melville, and James, so in our own times we see a number of writers whose works appear only slightly less important than those of Hemingway and Faulkner. Among these I would list: Sherwood Anderson, F. Scott Fitzgerald, Katherine Anne Porter, Caroline Gordon, Robert Penn Warren, and Eudora Welty. Of these, only the careers of Anderson and Fitzgerald are complete, and it may be that we are still too close to them to see the body of their work in its proper perspective. In addition, we have a generation of new writers whose careers may be said to have just begun: Walter Van Tilburg Clark, J. F. Powers, Peter Taylor, Wallace Stegner, Lionel Trilling, Irwin Shaw, Mark Schorer, Delmore Schwartz, and Truman Capote. Time will eliminate some of these names and add others. Their work is too new to fall within the bounds of literary history except as tentative manifestations of the present scene. It is beginning, however, to show itself rewarding to the literary critic, and it is upon the basis of work done by these authors (and others like them) that the attitudes of the second half of the century are likely to be founded.

Meanwhile, I think it no exaggeration to say that there has never been a time in the history of American literature when the practitioners of the short story have shown more interest in their craft. This has been indicated by the growth of short-story workshops at many of our leading universities and by the sponsoring of writers' conferences at others. It is reflected, too, in the evidence of careful workmanship which the stories by our youngest group of authors display as well as by an increasing concern with the problems of the short story in our critical journals. Indeed, as some readers maintain, the present decade may have become too doctrinaire in its approach. I would maintain only that it is too early to speak with assurance. Few generations have been noted for the accuracy with which they evaluated and recognized the genius of their contemporaries. Emerson and others of his time underrated Hawthorne. Melville's short stories went unnoticed for many years and have just recently been collected for the first time. Several of Henry James's most expert short stories and novels appeared during a period when his reputation was in decline. A recognition of these facts should humble even the most pretentious critic. Perhaps the most we can do is agree with Henry James, who, in making his case for the discussion of problems of fiction, said:

Art lives upon discussion, upon experiment, upon curiosity, upon variety of attempt, upon the exchange of views and the comparison of standpoints; and there is a presumption that those times when no one has anything to say about it, and has no reason to give for practice or preference, though they may be times of honor, are not times of development—are times, possibly even, of dulness.

FICTION AND REALITY:
1. THE NATURALISTS

THE chief differences in attitude among writers of fiction originate from a fundamental difference of opinion concerning the nature of reality. Hamlin Garland defined his own attitude as "the truthful statement of an individual impression corrected by reference to the fact." The fact was, of course, *natural* fact. Fundamentally, the attitude characterized by Garland placed its emphasis upon the natural materials of the writer. Garland wrote: "Obscurely forming in my mind were two great literary concepts —that truth was a higher quality than beauty, and that to spread the reign of justice should everywhere be the design and intent of the artist. The merely beautiful in art seemed petty, and success at the cost of the happiness of others a monstrous egotism." To understand the implications of such a statement we need to penetrate to the obviously intended meaning of such words as "truth" and "beauty." We need also to understand the seemingly logical relationships between the statement that "truth [is] a higher quality than beauty" and that the aim of the artist should be "to spread the reign of justice."

The question has to do with a significant philosophical problem. Truth, for Garland, was represented by the facts of the natural universe as they were conceived by nineteenth-century science. It was the artist's duty to reproduce these facts—this truth. Since life was not, as Darwin and others had shown, beautiful, neither should art be beautiful. So far as literature was concerned, beauty is represented by the facile and the decorative qualities of style and formal structure; so far as life is concerned, it is represented by the whole world of civilized manners. Style and manners, in Garland's view, obscured the painful truth of what he considered to be reality. Justice would, therefore, consist in revealing the cold, often hideous, face of the natural world.

Certainly it is difficult not to sympathize with such an aim; and particularly in the years following the predominance of the late Victorians and the Georgians in England and the superficial products of much genteel writing in America, such a program could not fail to appeal even to writers of greater talent and insight than Hamlin Garland. Thus, Stephen Crane could write in 1892:

I renounced the clever school in literature. It seemed to me that there must be something more in life than to sit and cudgel one's brains for the clever and witty expedients. So I developed all alone a little creed of art which I thought was a good one. Later I discovered that my creed was identical with the one of Howells and Garland and in this way I became involved in the beautiful war between those who say that art is man's substitute for nature and we are most successful in art when we approach the nearest to nature and truth.

We must remember, however, that Crane—as well as Howells and Garland—was primarily in rebellion against an excessive gentility in the writings of his time. We must remember also that Crane later became a great friend of both Henry James and Joseph Conrad, even a defender of James against the excessive prejudice and misunderstanding of less perceptive readers. Nevertheless, we must notice that at this point Crane equates nature with truth. We must believe, too, that what he meant by nature was very nearly what Garland considered it, not the more complicated view of Hawthorne with his "truths of the human heart," of Melville with his faith in "historic memory," or of James with his view that, though "Art deals with what we see . . . it has no sooner done this than it has to take account of a process," a means of dealing with the strong mixture which goes to make up character.

But though Garland, Crane, and Howells mark the beginning of naturalistic fiction in America, they belong really to the nineteenth century. In the present century, the writers who seem best to fit this admittedly and necessarily loose category would be: Frank Norris, Jack London, Theodore Dreiser, Sherwood Anderson, Ring Lardner, Erskine Caldwell, James T. Farrell, and John Steinbeck. With the exception of Ring Lardner, and with the possible exception of Sherwood Anderson, however, these authors' reputations are based principally upon their novels. Also, these novels, whatever their virtues, were not characterized by careful craftsmanship and technical competence, but rather by bold portrayals of life and by rigid social and political attitudes. Life was nature, not the superficial manners of the genteel tradition. Society was frontier life or life in the slums of the large cities or life in the environs of American industry. Politics was rebellion against a growing industrialism and a capitalistic economy, against economic and social injustice. Behind much of this was the rapid postwar expansion of business and industry which spurred the growth of radical philosophies and reform movements. Such movements were reflected by the muckraking journalism of the first quarter of the century and by the proletarian writing which followed the stock-market crash of 1929. Their culture heroes were not literary figures so much as they were scientists, pseudo philosophers, and politicians. They were such figures as François Fourier, Charles Darwin, Henry George, Herbert Spencer, Thorstein Veblen, and Karl Marx. They were modernists as opposed to traditionalists. At their worst, writers were reformers first and only secondarily literary men. At their best, they were artists despite their views. The most extreme, if not the most completely characteristic, example of this fact is Frank Norris, whose present reputation is based upon three novels: *McTeague* (1899), *The Octopus* (1901), and *The Pit* (1903), the latter published a year following its author's untimely death at the age of thirty-two. Although Norris published what have been called "stories and sketches," none of these survives today. They were collected from the files of *The Wave*, a San Francisco literary weekly, in 1931, during the flurry of interest occasioned by the economic depression of the 1930's, but none of them found its way into permanent collections. They have been, so far as literary interest is concerned, forgotten—and rightly so.

Jack London, on the other hand, although his reputation has declined greatly since the years following the end of World War I, is still to be found in many standard short-story anthologies. London was born in San Francisco in 1876 and published his first volume of short stories *The Son of the Wolf, Tales of the Far North* in 1900. In the years following, until his death in 1916, he published more than fifty volumes. The best of his short stories were issued by Sun Dial Press in a special edition in 1945 *(Best Short Stories of Jack London)*. His early stories were set in the Klondike region of Alaska which he visited during the period of the gold rush. Others reflect his experiences as a fisherman in the waters around San Francisco, his travels into the South Pacific, and his constant interest in social conditions. The bulk of them are vitiated by conformance to the timid requirements of his commercial markets, but a strong interest in nature, a background of wide experience as a traveler, and a consistent point of view gave his work a substance lacking in most popular fiction of his time. As Carl Van Doren wrote in *The American Novel:*

His heroes, whether wolves or dogs or prize-fighters or sailors or adventurers-at-large, have all of them approximately the same instincts and the same careers. They rise to eminence by battle, hold the eminence for a while by the same methods, and eventually go down under the rush of stronger enemies. London, with the strength of the strong, exulted in the struggle for survival. He saw human history in terms of the evolutionary dogma, which to him seemed a glorious, continuous epic, of which his stories were episodes. He set them in localities where the struggle could be most obvious: in the wilds of Alaska, on remote Pacific islands, on ships at sea out of hearing of the police, in industrial communities during strikes, in the underworlds of various cities, on the routes of vagabondage.

Yet London differs from Norris in that most of his stories survive today as simple adventure stories in books for young boys or in high-school anthologies. He was part of the current of naturalism at the beginning of the century, not a highly self-conscious force behind it. Even though Norris's stories are forgotten, his influence is not. Norris was an outspoken disciple of Emile Zola. Like Garland, too, he was a conscious and outspoken critic of social conditions.

There is no doubt, [he wrote shortly before his death] that the estate of American letters is experiencing a renaissance. Formality, the old idols, the demi-gorgons and autocrats no longer hold an absolute authority. A multitude of false gods are clamoring for recognition, shouldering one another about to make room for their altars, soliciting incense as if it were patronage. No doubt these "draw many after them," but the "nature revival" has brought the galvanizing, vital element into this tumult of little inkling sham divinities and has shown that life is better than "literature," even if the "literature" be of human beings and the life be that of a faithful dog.

As a reader for a New York publisher, Norris recognized his own values in the first novel of Theodore Dreiser and secured the publication of *Sister Carrie* (1900). Whatever attitude we take toward the renaissance of naturalism which Garland and Norris recognized at the turn of the century, we must recognize that Norris was an active and moving spirit behind it. Jack London was not, not because he disagreed with the essential attitudes behind it, but because he was basically a professional craftsman; and limited though his standards of craftsmanship were, they succeeded in portraying isolated and episodic fragments of life with a sense of value, less limited than the laborious case histories of Norris's short stories, limited otherwise than even the best of Theodore Dreiser's short stories are limited.

For technically and ideologically, Dreiser is in the mainstream of American naturalism running from Garland, through Norris and Dreiser, to James T. Farrell. London is nearer the more ambiguous position of Stephen Crane, a position which, basically sympathetic to the ideology of naturalism, differs from it primarily in the degree to which it acknowledges the demands, first, of craftsmanship, then, of traditional literature—differs in the degree to which it acknowledges the significance of James's process. Strangely enough (or perhaps "naturally enough"), the degree to which some form of literary discipline is acknowledged usually represents the degree in which the stories of London are superior to the stories of Norris. Likewise, the superiority of Sherwood Anderson to Dreiser as a writer of short stories, or the superiority of Steinbeck, Caldwell, and Lardner to James T. Farrell, lies not in the social consciousness of each, not in the element of rebellion against traditional social or moral values, but in the technical superiority of each as a literary craftsman. In short, these writers may be said to share the limitations of naturalism (their subject matter) while differing in the degree in which they accept or reject the technical means of controlling their material.

Theodore Dreiser, when asked once why he did not write more short stories, is reported to have said, "I need a large canvas." There are technical reasons why this is so. Many of his stories are not so much short stories as they are case histories, episodes, or what seem to be outlines for longer works. Although he published five volumes of short works, not all of them even pretend to be short stories in the accepted sense. Two are portraits. One includes so-called short novels. His best stories are contained in two volumes: *Free,* published in 1918, containing "The Lost Phoebe," "The Second Choice," "Old Rogaum and His Theresa," and the title story, all of which are among those most frequently read today; and *Chains,* published in 1927, which contains "The Hand," "Chains," and "Typhoon," the last considered by F. O. Matthiessen "one of Dreiser's most powerful stories."

The adjective "powerful" has been most frequently used

by critics and reviewers to describe the effects of Dreiser's work. Lionel Trilling is certainly right when he objects to the imprecision with which the word is commonly used. But such imprecision is a reflection of the extended nature of both the subject matter and the method of Dreiser. His principal effects are the result of accumulation, and in his novels this massive movement of accretion succeeds in portraying the large, imprecise movement of a whole society in flux. Although Dreiser did occasionally attempt literary devices which would focus upon individual characters and situations, such devices succeed only in the novels where the larger panorama dwarfs the artificiality of the individual portrait and makes criticism of it appear petty. The novel, while it has a tradition of manners, has also the tradition of history, and history is, in one sense at least, accumulative in the manner that Dreiser's novels are. The short story, however, is too brief to accommodate itself wholly to this effect, and Dreiser lacked the technical facility to control it even partially.

Theodore Dreiser was born into an impoverished Middle Western family in 1871. His upbringing by a stern Roman Catholic father, whose inability to earn a living forced the family to move often from place to place, left Dreiser with a hatred for the demanding and, to him, meaningless and ineffective forms of his inherited religion. His painful childhood experiences gave him an understanding and a fear of the abject poverty possible in American society. His personal philosophy developed from an early interest in the writings of Herbert Spencer and a growing interest in science as a means of understanding and controlling social action. Concepts of individual morality were bound to the larger, over-all concept of man in a society where the artificial restraints of wealth and social position were removed, where economic equality was achieved, and where the chemical urges of the blood were observed and respected.

Although Dreiser had, as Sherwood Anderson also had, a period of moderate and respectable success, his rebellion against respectability was less self-conscious than Anderson's. When literary success came to him in the 1920's and the early 1930's, however, his greater prestige as a writer dramatized the rebellion in a way that Anderson's never did. Also, it paved the way for a similar success by the writers of greater talent and more rigorous training who were to follow.

Dreiser's ideas were no more precisely or clearly formulated than were his concepts of his craft. Nevertheless, there are certain primary beliefs which become clear as a result of the reading of his articles, short stories, and novels. Chief among these was the belief that evil in man resulted not so much from an inherent tendency for evil in the individual as it came from the unreasonable and often unjust demands of a society organized to favor the well-to-do and enslave the poor. What was tolerated on one level of society was punished on the other. He stated once that one of his principal reasons for writing was the hope that, by revealing true social conditions, he could stimulate a move for their reform. His later interest in communism and in the Quakers suggests two of the means by which he felt reform could be accomplished. Yet, there was more Darwinism in him than social optimism, so that he viewed life as a struggle for survival more than as a struggle for Utopia, and it is this view, no doubt, which kept him a writer. Only seldom did he crusade for his own literary views (most notably when he sued the motion-picture producer of *An American Tragedy* for misrepresentation), and his biographical writings suggest that he viewed his craft, in part at least, as his principal means of satisfying the drive of his own ego.

Almost any of Dreiser's stories might have been expanded into novels, for they are, as a rule, confined neither in space nor in time. They are seldom based upon incidents, or when they are, the incidents are usually culminating events in a long series of injustices, misunderstandings, and intolerances which must be rehearsed in order to lend credibility to what is generally a final catastrophe. Their themes are not, as a rule, embedded in the material and thus revealed and illuminated through the media of style, structure, and character development. Dreiser does not possess themes so much as he presents a theme: a constantly recurring suggestion that the world is out of joint and that this disjointure might be set aright by the achieving of social justice. His stories, thus, are not so much a bodying forth of his theme as they are a repetitive illustration of it. His characters, which in his longer works with their greater space and more leisurely pace can be developed roundly and believably and so achieve a kind of wholeness in their own rights, remain too often sketchy and insubstantial in his stories. His tone, substantiated in his novels by the accumulating sense of social oppression battering at man's weaknesses and limitations, cannot develop believably within the brief space of the short story and so leaves us with the sense of its having been faked or artifically induced.

An example of this is the story which Matthiessen calls powerful—"Typhoon." The suggested image of the title is not developed within the story, but it implies a corollary between the natural elements and human emotions. The principal figure, Ida Zobel, is raised in the strict and orderly household of her father, a German immigrant and a moderately prosperous small businessman. Denied the normal social relations of children her own age, Ida grows into a beautiful young girl unprotected by experience and knowledge of her own associates. She is repressed by fears of her strict father and stepmother but abnormally attracted by the seeming glitter of the world of romance. When she is finally allowed to keep company with a young man her own age, she becomes an easy object of sexual conquest. Naïvely surprised by the appearance of pregnancy, she is just as naïvely astonished when her young man, disregarding his words of love and endearment, refuses the responsibility of marriage. She has become merely another of his youthful conquests. Caught between the pressure of her own ignorance and her fear of her father, she finally determines to force the boy to fulfill his promises. Taking an old revolver from her father's desk at the store, she faces her lover and demands that he marry her. When he refuses, her emotions force her into the act of killing but do not allow her to turn the gun on herself as she had intended. She is taken into custody, protected by society during the term of pregnancy, tried, and acquitted. The implications here are that had either society or her stern parent taken the proper precautions, tragedy would have been averted. As it is, a thoughtless but essentially good young man has been killed, Ida's father has been forced to move his business to a new location, Ida herself has only the dreariest and most unhappy view of the future. Marked by the tragedy, she considers herself a social outcast. As a person, she has no values upon which to build a new life. In despair, finally, she returns to the scene of her seduction at King Lake Park "and calmly stepping to the water and wading out to her knees—to her waist—her breasts—in the mild caressing water—and then to her lips and over them—and finally, deliberately—conclusively—sinking beneath its surface and without a cry or sigh."

The weakness of this story consists first of all in the over-simplicity of the concept. The events themselves are plausible; they are such as might be reported almost any day in the daily newspaper. The motivation of the act by which Ida Zobel ruins her life is understandable. Yet, as Dreiser tells the story, there is little indication that any part of the responsibility rests with Ida. She is, first of all, the result of a home environment which has withheld her from life, so that when she faces its risks and is betrayed, it is the society which has provided such an environment which is to blame. Likewise, the sophistication of her seducer is not so much the result of a limitation of character but rather the result of society's failure to develop virtues inherent in the boy; and these are represented less as the natural virtue of the passively innocent than they are the qualities of aggression and competition which Dreiser saw as the first law of nature. The events of the story are designed to occur with the mechanical consistency of a chemical process—to apply one of the author's most frequent analogies. The short story is a report to society of an incident which the author sees as inevitable, granted the initial conditions in the education of the principal characters.

Even if we admit the general rightness of such a concept as a means of looking at life, we must also recognize the incompleteness of it. Such events are usually complicated by subtle differences of character which help to explain why not all girls of Ida Zobel's upbringing murder their lovers and then commit suicide. If the facts of Ida's experience are true, therefore, they are but half-true. Also, Dreiser's treatment of the history leaves out an examination of the sense of individual responsibility which would have occurred to an author more concerned with the psychological implications of the action, less confined by a concept so rigid as Dreiser's simple determinism. The story as it now stands tells us only that Ida Zobel saw no way out of her despair. There is little indication that she experienced any emotion not directly related to herself and her own predicament, no compassion, remorse, pride, or even personal guilt.

The importance of such an attitude to us here is that, seeing life as simple, mechanical, and deterministic, Theodore Dreiser would naturally see little need for the techniques by which other authors have attempted to convey the impression of density and complexity so essential to a true picture of human experience. Dreiser's methods are, therefore, in a very real sense antiliterary. Insofar as he was conscious of his aims, they would appear to be more practical than contemplative, rather propagandistic than contributing to a true experience of the imagination. They leave the reader, as Virginia Woolf said of the novels of Arnold Bennett, more likely to feel the urge to sit down and write a check—to engage actively in some movement of reform—than to experience either the emotional exaltation or the penetrating illumination usually associated with the most important works of literary art.

Dreiser's courtships end in betrayal, his marriages in failure, his business enterprises either in bankruptcy or in an ironic success to be posed against personal moral and emotional bankruptcy. The causes of such failures lie in society's unreasonable (and unreal) demands, in the inability of parents to understand the natural desires and inclinations of their children, or in the false idealism with which his characters attempt to face the harsh realities of life. As is the case with writing aimed, consciously or unconsciously, partially or wholly, toward social reform, many of Dreiser's situations now seem dated, more the result of the particular social conditions of the time against which he protested

than the result of an inherent and timeless quality of character. Thus, when social reform is accomplished, the basic
situation of most of Dreiser's short stories is altered and
little remains except the quaint speech of his characters
(" 'Oh, sure, sure, it was all right, only what do you think
I'm made of? Say, have a heart, I'm human, ain't I? I've got
some feelings same as anybody else. Ain't I crazy about you
and ain't you crazy about me? Well, then—besides—well,
say . . .' ") and the sense that they only imagine themselves
to be trapped, for many of the specific evils against which
they are signs of protest have been altered by time—childhood education, marriage, investment control, working
hours, etc. In "Typhoon," for instance, it is difficult to understand the inevitability of Ida Zobel's suicide, because it
has become almost impossible to conceive of the particular
blindness of both society and the parents of Ida and Edward, except in terms of the time in which the story was
written. Which is to say that in a short story such as this
one, Dreiser did not succeed in penetrating beyond the
temporal limitations of his characters and his situation to
the universal limitations which underlie all human acts.

Dreiser's best-known short story "The Lost Phoebe" is
deservedly more popular, because it succeeds—as most of his
stories do not—in getting at this essential quality of human
existence. It is primarily the story of old Henry Reifsneid-
er's attempt to face a life of loneliness, bereft of his children,
who have left to make their lives elsewhere than on the old
Midwestern farm, and of his wife, Phoebe, who died when
he had reached the age of seventy. There is social comment
in the portrayal of conditions on the farm and in the implied
reasons why the children left, apparently feeling no ties to
the farm or to their parents. There are traces of Dreiser's
characteristic method in the lengthy and generalized filling

in of the family background. There are stylistic lapses in the author's familiar attempt to handle the intricacies of rural dialogue almost wholly through a phonetic representation of sounds, with too little hearing of the essential rhythms and a poor eye for traditional folk images. Yet the central situation, in which Henry imagines his wife to have returned, in which he attempts to recover the small comfort of her companionship by dissolving into a world of fantasy, is moving in its natural pathos and psychologically right in its implications of small tragedy. The scenes in which Henry wanders the countryside calling for his "lost Phoebe" are moving in a way in which Ida Zobel's more violent history is not. The conclusion, in which Henry is lured to his death by the vision of his wife, is closer to folk legend than it is to social theory, and it thus picks up and encloses psychological truths which reach beyond the action of the immediate scene. In these respects, it is nearer to the better work of Stephen Crane, Sherwood Anderson, and John Steinbeck than it is to the bulk of Dreiser's short fiction or to the works of the author who most resembles Dreiser, James T. Farrell.

Farrell was born in Chicago in 1904. He, too, came from a rather poor Roman Catholic family, and he, too, rebelled against the strictness of his upbringing, seeing his religion primarily as a social force preserved as a means of enslaving the poor. His works are also characterized by their length (his principal works being a trilogy of Chicago boyhood, *Studs Lonigan*), a looseness of style, and a preoccupation with the portrayal of social conditions. While Farrell has written many short stories, they are even less formally constructed than Dreiser's, more strictly clinical histories. While the best of his novels achieve an authentic sense of the brutality and waste of life in the urban slums, his short stories usually present only the horror and pathos of a particular instance. Although he has acknowledged the necessity for critical standards of a literary nature in his written criticism, Farrell seems incapable of conceiving an essential unity of subject matter and literary technique. His short stories thus become mere instances illustrating his particular view of social illness. They fail, finally, to demonstrate either the social complexity of Dreiser or Crane or the psychological complexity of John Steinbeck or Sherwood Anderson.

Sherwood Anderson was born in Camden, Ohio, in 1876, the third child in a family never far from real poverty. His first book did not appear until 1916, because Anderson had begun his career as a moderately successful middle-class businessman and he did not begin to write seriously until he had grown weary of his seemingly futile occupation. His first stories were published in *The Dial*, *The Seven Arts*, and *The Little Review*, his first book collection being *Winesburg, Ohio* in 1919, followed by *The Triumph of the Egg* in 1921. Later volumes include: *Horses and Men* (1923), *Hands and Other Stories* (1925), *Alice, and the Lost Novel* (1929), and *Death in the Woods and Other Stories* (1933).

Anderson's principal subject matter was small-town life in the Middle West, much of it based on his own experience and colored by the revolt against what he considered a false respectability. He was an acknowledged admirer of Dreiser. However, his restrictions against the inhibiting quality of middle-class American life was based much more fully on the new psychoanalysis than was Dreiser's, and its basis was thus psychological rather than economic. When he concerned himself with economic factors, it was to show how they reflected in the individual psyche, not in an aggregate society or in the relations of social classes.

Yet even this interest in psychoanalysis was nonprofessional and impressionistic, a substantiation of his own romantic views concerning the relationship of man to nature. Anderson saw the growing industrialization of America as moving hand in hand with a developing artificiality of social customs and manners. His characters are tortured by social restrictions from which they can be freed only by a return to nature, a trusting of their instincts and natural sensibilities. His world, like the world of nineteenth-century romanticism, depended upon his faith in a natural moral order which could be known only after the artificial layers of social and religious custom had been removed or penetrated by a childlike intuition.

Like the naturalists, Anderson saw in nature the ultimate reality, whether it be reality in a material or in a moral sense. But as a writer of short stories, he depends very little upon such views, at least in his most successful works. As a craftsman, he is perhaps nearer to Stephen Crane, an impressionist, than he is to Theodore Dreiser. Anderson did not so much despise his craft as he emphasized the necessity of catching the natural, rhythmic flow of life. His works are not formal in the sense that James's stories are; neither are they formless as are the least successful stories of Dreiser. Their unity is, however, more thematic than structural. For the most part, they avoid the danger of becoming case histories. By concentrating upon his characters as individuals, he avoided, also, the need which Dreiser and Farrell felt for a large canvas, and he was thus more at home in the short-story form than most serious writers of his time and temperament. What later writers, such as Ernest Hemingway, rebelled against in him was a too naïve and uncritical faith in the goodness of human nature, an attitude which seemed, after the experiences of World War I, both excessively sentimental and fundamentally untrue. Yet at his best, in such

stories as "I Want to Know Why," "I'm a Fool," "The Egg,"
and "Seeds," Anderson is very close to them, both in manner and in subject matter. "I Want to Know Why" is probably as good as, perhaps better than, Hemingway's "My Old
Man." Certainly it is a similar kind of story, and the general
superiority of Hemingway to Anderson, both as novelist and
as short-story writer, depends upon a scope which is not only
wider than Anderson's but also more complex, more de-
tailed, and, therefore, perhaps more true to the whole of
experience. Likewise, such authors as Katherine Anne Porter, Robert Penn Warren, and William Faulkner seem conscious of facets of experience of which Sherwood Anderson
seemed almost totally unaware.

John Steinbeck, whose best-known novels (In Dubious
Battle and The Grapes of Wrath) were more sharply social
than were the novels of either Dreiser or Farrell, achieves,
in his best short stories, a measure of discipline impossible
to either by a psychological symbolism, often too broad and
approaching sentimentality, but at its best comparable to
the least self-conscious works of Sherwood Anderson. Steinbeck, who was born in California in 1902, has two similar
but sharply distinct manners in his novels, the pseudopas-
toral, folksy manner of Tortilla Flat and the note of social
protest of The Grapes of Wrath. The former manner domi-
nates his short stories, and it has come recently to be most
characteristic of his novels. In his best short stories, however, as in Anderson's, the underlying symbols achieve a control which, combined with his strongly emphasized themes,
proves more satisfying than the loosely constructed histories
of Dreiser and of Farrell. Such stories as "The Red Pony,"
"The Chrysanthemums," "The Harness," and "Johnny
Bear," while not among the best stories of the century, represent a serious attempt to celebrate the natural instincts of

man and to suggest agrarian values more satisfying than those in most of the regional writing produced during the same period. While John Steinbeck's reputation has declined since it reached its high point with the publication of *The Grapes of Wrath* in 1939, it has not suffered the almost complete neglect we see in the careers of such Midwestern regionalists as Willa Cather and Ruth Suckow; and it is likely that all of these authors (including Sherwood Anderson) deserve more serious attention than they are receiving today, if not as short-story writers of the first rank, at least as authors of a few extremely interesting and valuable works.

Concerning form, Sherwood Anderson wrote that "it is largely a matter of depth of feeling." At the conclusion of one of his most popular stories, "Death in the Woods," his narrator says: "A thing so complete has its own beauty." But such expressions need investigation. Ernest Hemingway, who began as a friend and admirer of Anderson, came to believe that Anderson's "depth of feeling" was faked; it was the result of loose thinking and loose writing: "If a man writes clearly enough any one can see if he fakes." It was not that Hemingway objected to the tone of mystery which Anderson so often evokes. "Mysticism," he said, "implies a mystery and there are many mysteries; but incompetence is not one of them; nor is overwritten journalism made literature by the injection of a false epic quality." At his worst, Anderson was undoubtedly guilty of making unjustified appeals on behalf of his characters. In such a story as "The New Englander," too much weight depends upon stock figures of animal sexuality, regional sexual inhibitions, the fertility of the soil, and the falling rain as a symbol of sexual gratification, without adequate exploration of the personal frustrations of the characters themselves; in such brief sketches as "Motherhood," "Senility," and "The Man in the Brown Coat" there is neither the incisiveness of allegory nor the completeness of character development or an enclosing action. Too much depends upon the atmosphere of social revolt, a revolt aimed particularly against the conventional taboos concerning sex. In the better stories, such as "Death in the Woods" and "I Want to Know Why," the sentimentality is avoided either by a controlled, ironic approach to the material or by an all-encompassing moral point of view which restricts and focuses the meaning of the events.

"Death in the Woods" tells the story of the death of an old woman, how her body, violated and imposed upon during life, became beautiful in death. It does not avoid sentimentality certainly, but the sentiment is controlled and held in bounds by the attitude of the young boy who narrates the story and by the events themselves. Anderson's own concept of the story emphasizes the sentiment: "It seems to me that the theme of this story is the persistent animal hunger of man. There are these women who spend their whole lives, rather dumbly feeding this hunger." The story seems rather an effort to define the nature and the appeal of beauty as it is recognized through the eyes of a young boy; in this sense, its tone avoids the risk of sentimentality. "The whole thing," Anderson says, "the story of the old woman's death, was to me as I grew older like music heard from far off. The notes had to be picked up slowly one at a time. Something had to be understood." The irony exists in the fact that the young boy recognizes the beauty without understanding it; yet it is clear that the author understood it. It is objectified in the frozen body of the old woman which becomes like that of a young girl, yet strangely devoid of sexual attraction. "It may have been the snow, clinging to the frozen flesh, that made it look so white and lovely, so like marble."

The dogs, though they had torn the bundle of meat from her shoulder and devoured it, had not touched her. They had simply removed the layer of old clothes which hid her beauty. Death, which is animal-like, had effaced the marks of hard labor and mistreatment which the woman had endured in life. Death, like the circling dogs, had framed and emphasized that which life had concealed. This is certainly not all that can be said about death, but so far as it goes it is true, and the story convinces us. We are less impressed by the mystery of it than by what it reveals.

Likewise, John Steinbeck's most popular story "The Chrysanthemums" has elements of sentimentality which are somehow held in check by the over-all concept and by the specific nature of the facts which the story reveals. It is based upon an assumed relationship between the fertile growth of plant life and physical violence and sexuality in human beings. Thirty-five-year-old Elisa Allen, a farmer's wife, is tending the flower beds on her place near Salinas when she is interrupted by an itinerant scissors sharpener and potmender, who travels yearly between Seattle and San Diego. She has nothing for him to mend and attempts to send him on his way. When he pretends an interest in her work with the chrysanthemums, however, she senses anew the mysterious power which she possesses in her "planter's hands." She talks eagerly with him about her flowers, and the author skillfully portrays the almost sexual attraction she feels for the old man and for the gypsy life he leads. He speaks about knowing someone down the road who has no chrysanthemums in her garden, and Elisa offers to send a plant with him. She also digs up two old discarded pots for him to mend. There is a similarity in Elisa's skill with her flowers and the man's skill with his mending tools which might have established a real bond between them, except

that the man had merely "pretended" an interest in Elisa's
flowers and Elisa had merely "made" work for the man—
work which she did not need done. Elisa does not discover
this until later. The man's interest stimulates the life in her
so that after he has left, when she is preparing to go to town
with her husband, "she tore off her soiled clothes and flung
them into the corner. And then she scrubbed herself with
a little block of pumice, legs and thighs, loins and chest and
arms, until her skin was scratched and red. When she had
dried herself she stood in front of a mirror in her bedroom
and looked at her body. She tightened her stomach and
threw out her chest." This intense physical awareness is
maintained until, when she is in the car riding to town with
her husband, she happens to see the plant she had so care-
fully prepared discarded along the highway. The vitality
which she has felt is suddenly frustrated by her awareness
of the potmender's insincerity, and she seeks to rechannel
it by suggesting to her husband that they go to the prize
fights in the town. Puzzled, he agrees. She, however, suddenly realizes the impossibility—the futility—of such an escape. The youthful energy and vitality she had felt is dis-
solved as she turns her head aside and breaks into tears,
"crying weakly—like an old woman."

The underlying assumption of an affinity between human passion and the rich soil of the land, which Anderson
uses sentimentally in "The New Englander," is here concretized through the brief relationship of Elisa Allen and
the old potmender. It does not carry the full burden of the
action, as it does in Anderson's story, but serves merely as
background to support the momentary awakening of passion in the controlled and ordinary life of Elisa. Its conception results from the romantic awareness of Steinbeck
of an underlying affinity between the natural life and hu-

man morality, but there is an exceptional control of that concept through the subtle application of commonly understood psychological principles concerning the freeing and frustrating of elemental passions. The poignancy of the end of the story results from Elisa's recognition that the passion (which was a worthy emotion in itself) had resulted from an unworthy cause—the potmender's insincere interest in her skill with her hands. An additional irony exists, however, in the reader's recognition that Elisa's false interest in the man's skill was also unworthy of his genuine craftsmanship.

A similar concept is behind one of Anderson's finest stories, the often reprinted "I Want to Know Why." The comparison here is between animal life and human morality, and there are three levels as seen through the sensibilities of the fifteen-year-old boy who tells the story. The first is the world of white gentility which, because of its concept of right and wrong, insulated the boy against the very things which seem to him to encompass the greatest beauty. The second is the world of the Negroes, particularly the race-track Negroes. "Often a white man you might meet, when you run away from home like that, might appear to be all right and give you a quarter or a half dollar or something, and then go right and give you away. White men will do that, but not a nigger. You can trust them. They are squarer with kids." The world of purest beauty is objectified in the thoroughbred race horse. "If you've never been crazy about thoroughbreds it's because you've never been around where they are much and don't know any better. They're beautiful. There isn't anything so lovely and clean and full of spunk and honest and everything as some race horses." The boy's admiration for the thoroughbred is transferred to the trainer who handles him: "I was thinking about Jerry Tillford the trainer and how happy he was all through the race. I liked him that afternoon even more

than I ever liked my own father. I almost forgot the horses
thinking that way about him. It was because of what I had
seen in his eyes as he stood in the paddocks beside Sunstreak
before the race started. I knew he had been watching and
working with Sunstreak since the horse was a baby colt, had
taught him to run and be patient and when to let himself
out and not to quit, never. I knew that for him it was like a
mother seeing her child do something brave or wonderful.
It was the first time I ever felt for a man like that."

The emotions aroused in the boy are similar to those
of Elisa Allen, both seeming to share an interest with another person, that interest raised to the intensity of passion
through the vitality and force of the "natural" occupation
which seemingly links them. But the boy is disillusioned as
Elisa was. His moment of revelation comes when he follows
Jerry Tillford to an old farmhouse after the race. He hears
Jerry brag. He hears him say that "he made that horse, that
it was him that won the race and made the record." He sees
Jerry's interest in the hard, unclean women in the house.
His disillusionment comes as a kind of initiation. Things
are different now. "At the tracks the air don't taste as good
or smell as good. It's because a man like Jerry Tillford, who
knows what he does, could see a horse like Sunstreak run,
and kiss a woman like that the same day. I can't make it out.
Darn him, what did he want to do like that for? I keep thinking about it and it spoils looking at horses and smelling
things and hearing niggers laugh and everything. Sometimes I'm so mad about it I want to fight someone. It gives
me the fantods. What did he do it for? I want to know why."

The weakness of this story, and it is weak only insofar as
it fails to become one of the great stories of the century, lies
probably in the weight that is given to the natural beauty
of the instinctive life led in the company of the thoroughbreds, with too little attention paid to the opposite side of

the problem. Here it is, I think, that Anderson's concept of his role as a reformer has limited the thematic development of his story material. There are indications that he sees a value in the boy's life apart from horses, Negroes, and the race track, even though the boy is primarily in rebellion against his too civilized home environment. But too little attention is paid to those values, so that in the end we are left with the sense of man's limitation, with too little understanding of what those limitations represent. "Things are different now." Some of the beauty is gone, because the boy has been forced to a recognition of the ugliness. We are forced to conclude that the ugliness is primarily an absence of the beautiful, or a distortion of it—or, to use one of Anderson's favorite words, a "grotesque." The grotesque is pathetic when viewed beside the possibility of beauty. Is this all he meant to say?

We do know that Anderson put little value upon formal beauty. His style is loose, but when related to the kinds of characters with which he most often dealt it is apt. He had a better ear than Dreiser for dialogue, a finer sensitivity to the shades of tone and atmosphere. Yet in formulating his artistic credo, he asked: "And if we are a crude and childlike people, how can our literature hope to escape the influence of that fact? Why indeed should we want to escape it?" But this is begging the question. The question should be: "Why have we chosen to put value on the crude and the childlike?" And further: "Even though we have put value upon natural, even primitive qualities, does this mean that our art should be crude and childlike?" There is, of course, a sense in which an uninspired respect for form vitiates any art; but it is equally true that an unrestricted faith in pure sensitivity has a similar effect. Anderson's style at its best is not so much crude as it is smooth; at its worst it is less childlike than it is aesthetically pretentious. His structure does not merely give the impression of ease and looseness; it *is* easy and loose. Melville could catch the element of crudity and childlikeness in the American character in a work as planned and orderly as *Moby Dick*. So could Mark Twain at his best, and *Huckleberry Finn* is a much more orderly work than many readers have been willing to admit. The order in these works resulted from the authors' conceptions of the problem of form and content, their awareness of the need to reconcile in some degree the values of civilized manners with the virtues of an active life in the natural surroundings of a frontier society.

Anderson's limitations would seem to exist primarily in the emphasis which he felt to be necessary in order to dramatize his revolt against the world of genteel manners. His grotesque characters existed in terms of this revolt and were thus too often truly grotesques (that is, pathetic rather than tragic figures), struggling to exert their virtues with too little regard for their limitations, unfortified by an underlying philosophy which might have added the dimension of reality to them. Had he gone deeper into the psychological motivation of his characters as he seemed on the brink of doing in "Seeds," he might have achieved the more genuine pathos of Thomas Mann. Had he been less solemn in his approach, his characters might have achieved the meaningful distortion of the truly comic, as indeed the figure of the father almost does in "The Egg." For Anderson was never far removed from the tradition of native American humor. He was merely insulated against its final, and finest, effect— the quixotic application of the standards of sophisticated society in the raw, utilitarian world of the frontier, an application which might have disclosed both the virtues and the limitations of both worlds; that is, have achieved a more complete and genuine spirit of reform.

It seems likely that the spirit of reform is at the bottom

of most comedy, but it is a spirit which must rise from the body of the work, not exist outside and behind it, forcing it toward a preconceived end. Erskine Caldwell, whose finest works are predominantly comic in tone, often fails to encompass and enclose his material in the same way that Anderson did. He succeeds best, however, as in *Tobacco Road* (1932) and *God's Little Acre* (1933), when he presents his rural Southerners with the characteristic vigor and lustiness of the traditional rustic. He fails most utterly when he attempts a novel of sociopolitical protest, such as *All Night Long* (1942), which he subtitled *A Novel of Guerrilla Warfare in Russia,* and which is obviously intended to depict his protest against Nazi brutality during the Russian invasion. Although few of his short stories succeed as well as the best of his novels, they illustrate the same extremes of success and failure. A native of Georgia where he was born in 1903, Erskine Caldwell has written of the life he knew as a boy among the poor whites and the Negroes, and his most persistent theme is the brutality of Southern agrarian society in its attempt to preserve a decayed social system.

Insofar as bulk is concerned, Caldwell is undoubtedly the most prolific writer among the moderns. He is what his most sympathetic critics persist in calling "a born story-teller." Henry Seidel Canby places him squarely in "the Mark Twain tradition": "Indeed in these tales, and others which throb with indignation against a maladjusted world in spite of the horse-play and mock innocence on top, Caldwell is Mark Twain's spiritual heir." But there is a significant difference between Mark Twain and Erskine Caldwell. In Twain's most bitterly ironic stories such as "The Mysterious Stranger," "Captain Stormfield's Visit to Heaven," and "The Man That Corrupted Hadleyburg" there is a well-defined and at least partly defensible skepticism always before the reader. Caldwell's stories of social protest come to depend too often upon an obscure, because badly defined, concept of some future corrective judgment. Thus, in what is perhaps his most respected short story "Kneel to the Rising Sun," the author finally reaches outside the story for a sentimental conclusion, a view of "the round red sun," which somehow, by its warmth, gave Lonnie, the principal character in the story, strength to rise to his feet after a night of violent injustice. The sun is obviously symbolic, but its use as the climactic symbol (fortified by its use in the title) is not necessarily the result of the major events which have come before. The promise of life-giving warmth is not a promise of mere physical regeneration but a promise of something for which "the round red sun" stands in the author's mind, perhaps the rising sun of social revolution: the dispossessed kneel, like Lonnie, beaten to the earth, but facing the regenerative warmth of social reform. If this interpretation is correct, then the symbol serves to transform a skillfully told story of betrayal into a tract asserting faith in a particular solution to the problem of social justice. For the story is really concerned with the effects of injustice upon the natural instincts for friendship and loyalty between two men of different races. If this interpretation is incorrect, then the symbol is obscure and too much attention is focused upon it.

The relationship between Twain and Caldwell, despite Mr. Canby's statement, exists primarily in those stories in which the least throb of indignation against a maladjusted world is evident, for Erskine Caldwell's most common method is the technique of traditional American humor—the tall tale. The Handsome Brown stories, "A Country Full of Swedes," "Candy-Man Beechum," and "Hamrick's Polar Bear" all depend upon grotesque distortions and exaggerations of character and incident told with a quiet understatement. This is the technique Twain raised to a high point in

Huckleberry Finn but which in many of his minor works represents little more than an intensification of a typical frontier attitude toward nineteenth-century concepts of nature and society, at best a genuine reflection of his time, at worst merely an extended joke. Neither Caldwell nor Twain is as successful in his short stories as he is in his best novels. And yet the situation here is somewhat different than in the case of Dreiser or of James T. Farrell. Humor can be accomplished in a short space if it is planned and incisive—highly self-conscious. When it is not, when it is improvisatory or when it is allied to broad social concepts, either it tends to become mere pointless entertainment or it demands time to construct a believable background of setting, character, and social myth. *Huckleberry Finn* and *Tobacco Road* provide this more leisurely development, but the majority of Erskine Caldwell's short stories do not.

Ring Lardner, who was born in Niles, Michigan, in 1885 and whose literary apprenticeship was served as a newspaperman, primarily in the Midwest, seems to belong more genuinely to the tradition of the native American humorists than does Caldwell. His use of the first-person narrator who uses jumbled syntax, misspellings, mispronunciation, and those remarks betraying an ironic intention far beyond his own conception reminds us of the creations of Artemus Ward, John Phoenix, and Josh Billings, and of the inferior works of Twain. The grandparent of such a character is, as Constance Rourke has pointed out, the Yankee pedlar of colonial times, from whom descended such rustics as the Yankee Jonathan of Royall Tyler's *The Contrast* and a host of naïve, ignorant, but natively shrewd Americans who paraded through the columns of such periodicals as *The Brickbat*, *The Jolly Joker*, and *Merryman's Monthly* during the mid-nineteenth century. Lardner's intentions, consciously or unconsciously, were, however, almost the exact opposite of those of the frontier humorists. While the characters of the pedlar, Jonathan, Davy Crockett, and Twain's "innocents" were essentially well-intentioned and shrewd, seeing through the pretenses of respectable society, Lardner's characters disclosed an underlying evil, not only in themselves but in the society from which they came. Their manner, instead of being a means of penetrating the mask of social manners, became itself a mask only slightly disguising a serious social illness lying beneath the surface. Whereas, too, the characters of the frontier humorists had been, for the most part, illiterate figures, inherently good, the characters of Lardner's stories were "urban clodhoppers" or, to him, members of the ignorant middle classes, disclosing through their innocence and pretended respectability a genuine and frightening cruelty, all the more cruel because it was clothed in the rags of romantic virtue.

It is undoubtedly no accident that the high point in Ring Lardner's popularity came during the late thirties when he was rediscovered (he had died in 1933) by a society highly critical of the social conditions which had led to the stock-market crash of 1929 and the ensuing years of depression. It was no accident, either, that these years marked the high point in Erskine Caldwell's critical reputation. Caldwell's popular reputation, which has increased since the advent of pocket-size books, resembles the popular reputations of the earlier humorists; and it is based, as theirs were, upon the pure entertainment value, spiced, in the case of Caldwell, with a preoccupation with the lusty sexuality of his Southern Negroes and poor whites.

There is no doubt that the qualities which raised Mark Twain's work to a rank commensurate with the works of Hawthorne and Melville were qualities inherent in the folk concepts and the language of the frontier, whether that frontier began at the Atlantic Coast, the Alleghenies, or the Mississippi River. It is a quality which is still to be found in the tone, the style, and the thematic matters of all of our best writers from Emerson through Hawthorne, Melville, and Walt Whitman to Ernest Hemingway, William Faulkner, Robert Penn Warren, and Eudora Welty. But it is a quality which is successful, as in the case of Mark Twain's best works, only when it is combined with an honest attempt to explore the nature of human experience, not fit it into a preconceived mold. If the characteristics which marked the naturalists in the American short story represented no more than a rebellion against social, economic, and political injustice, there would be little reason to make this a basis for literary evaluation. At their best such authors combined their anger and frustration with a penetrating insight into the true complexity of modern life. At their worst, they accepted an oversimple and too rigid optimism as a basic assumption from which to approach the problems of their craft. They served a laudable purpose insofar as they corrected the soft-minded, easy romanticism of the genteel tradition, insofar, even, as they assisted in the various phases of social reform. But the extreme of Clarence Darrow's concepts of social responsibility and the human will are no less one-sided than are the views of William Jennings Bryan, whom he opposed at the Scopes trial during the heyday of the literary naturalists. Such concepts are, in any event, only indirectly the concerns of art. For, while philosophies vie for precedence, the subject matter of literature may vary but the general approach to it must not. And to the majority of the present generation it has become a truism that literature—and this includes the short story—represents its own means of viewing the nature of reality.

FICTION AND REALITY:
2. THE TRADITIONALISTS

THE first reaction against naturalism in the short story was not an organized or highly self-conscious revolt. It cannot be said to be a literary movement. It developed concurrently with the regionalism of the 1920's and the social consciousness of the 1930's, and it drew what it needed from these sources, was often confused with them, and did not bother for a long time to deny its connections. It sprang most directly from the expatriation and the bohemianism of the years immediately preceding the depression. Its attitudes were, on the whole, international rather than regional; its aims, an examination of the morality of its times as well as a perfection of its craftsmanship. In a practical sense it differed from naturalism less in the amount of emphasis it put upon problems of truth—of morality and ideas—than it did in the emphasis it put upon such traditional concepts as historic legend, the psychology of myth, and the import of social manners. In short, its view of what constituted reality was at once broader and less a direct break with the past than were the views of naturalism.

What distinguished these writers as a group, however, is not merely the manner in which they differed from their predecessors but also the means by which they profited from the long line of literary tradition, applying the lessons of the past to a form which had up to this time scarcely achieved definition. From the past they recovered the concept of man as a heroic and tragic figure, thus substituting skepticism and irony for the wishful optimism of the nineteenth century, and they re-established the view that art was not merely an adjunct of morality or social progressivism. If they differ in these respects from the naturalists they may be said to have learned much from them, and what they learned added a new life and vitality to the older concepts. First of all, they learned a new frankness and honesty in the treatment of their subject matter. Secondly, they learned the importance of social change as a force in the experience of our times.

On the whole, however, such views were not held self-consciously, nor were they grasped completely by any single writer of these years. Evidence of their existence does not come from critical manifestoes or literary autobiography; rather, it comes from our present view of the intentions of the works produced. The era 1920 to 1940 produced, exclusive of the works discussed in the preceding chapter, such excellent short stories as Ernest Hemingway's "The Short Happy Life of Francis Macomber," "The Killers," "The Snows of Kilimanjaro," "The Capital of the World," "My Old Man," and "The Undefeated"; William Faulkner's "A Rose for Emily," "That Evening Sun," "Delta Autumn,"

"Spotted Horses," and "The Bear"; F. Scott Fitzgerald's "The Rich Boy," "May Day," and "Babylon Revisited"; Katherine Anne Porter's "Flowering Judas," "Old Mortality," "Maria Concepción," and "Pale Horse, Pale Rider"; Caroline Gordon's "Old Red" and "Her Quaint Honor"; Glenway Wescott's "The Pilgrim Hawk"; Kay Boyle's "White Horses of Vienna"; and Robert Penn Warren's "Blackberry Winter."

Compared with any similar period in the history of the American short story here is abundance indeed. If we examine this abundance two facts become immediately apparent: first, the remarkable number of fine stories produced by writers of the deep South; second, a remarkable unity of interest, often masked by a seeming difference in technical approach, which all of these authors have in common. An explanation for the eminence of Southern fiction during these years will be offered later. More important here are the specific similarities of attitude which bind these authors together and differentiate them from the authors discussed in the preceding chapter.

The aims of both Ernest Hemingway and William Faulkner were for a long time confused with those of the naturalists. Hemingway had said that the old ideals should be re-examined and reappraised. What he meant, as his work will testify, was not that they should be denied and discarded but rather that they should be stripped of the disguise with which an abstract idealism had clothed them, that they should be renewed by an artistic revelation of their relationship to the objects and the events of the immediate present—the violence of war and the disillusionment of apparent corruption and chaos. His subject matter cut through the taboos of genteel society and genteel editorship to discover a world of violence and seeming disorder, but a world struggling to define itself by codes similar in many respects to the old verities—the traditional decorum—of an older society. In his short stories his method worked in two directions, so that he could view the events of a modern bullfight or the hunt for big game as a classic revival of man's willful and heroic pitting himself against death; he could, at the same time. see the actions of the Roman soldiers who cast lots for Christ's garments at the time of the crucifixion in terms of the actual attitudes, events, and language of the modern soldier.

The specific works of Ernest Hemingway and William Faulkner will be considered in detail in a separate chapter. Their relevance to the present chapter consists in their importance in establishing attitudes and developing themes which were to become the central preoccupation of the years during which their major stories were produced. William Faulkner's interests were not different from Ernest Hemingway's, but his awareness of his own Southern historical background provided him with a concrete example of both the fallacious romanticism and the classic heroism of the past. His works are rooted in that background and represent an examination of it in terms of the shifting conditions of modern society, not unlike Ernest Hemingway's, but in some respects more satisfying. It possessed the means of objectifying both the past and the present in terms of Southern history, not only the broad contrast of pre-Civil War and post-Civil War society but in all its subtle development from the days of settlement through its grand period of aristocratic pretensions and into its postwar decay and transition.

Perhaps the chief difference between Ernest Hemingway and William Faulkner is represented by Ernest Hemingway's apparent deracination, William Faulkner's strong sense of regional background. That this difference exists cannot be denied. That it is less great than has often been assumed, however, can be indicated by suggesting that while Ernest Hemingway's best stories are set in an area far removed from the Middle West in which he grew up, his earliest stories were not, and all of his works reflect the sensibilities of characters who are the product of that environment, who were conditioned by the ceremony of hunting and fishing in the woods of Michigan (later Wyoming and Montana) or by the less pronounced decorum of Midwestern life. As it does exist, the difference is perhaps more pronounced in other authors of the same period, such authors as Kay Boyle, Glenway Wescott, and Conrad Aiken, the first a product of Minnesota, the second of Wisconsin, and the third a strange mixture of the South and of New England; or authors such as Caroline Gordon, whose subject matter is almost aggressively Southern, and Robert Penn Warren, whose subject matter is at least as exclusively Southern as Faulkner's. Both F. Scott Fitzgerald on the one hand and Katherine Anne Porter on the other have been more successful (at least in the best of their short stories) in preserving the kind of objectivity characterized by Faulkner and Hemingway. Katherine Anne Porter preserves her Southern identity as a convenient point of observation for the examination of events occurring in Europe, Mexico, and the Far West, as well as for an examination of her own Southern past. F. Scott Fitzgerald's characteristic voice is that of the Midwesterner confronted by the wealth, the sophistication, the manners of Eastern and European society, particularly in the hectic period during and following the fallacious prosperity of the 1920's.

On the whole, then, the differences are overshadowed by the similarity of interest and intention. Both the regionalism of the Southerners and the deracination of those authors who have come from other areas have been stressed too greatly in the past. Even two minor figures of the period, such as William Saroyan and William Carlos Williams, exhibit like differences and similarities; and to say as much is perhaps as far as one should go in attempting to fit any of these authors into one Procrustean bed; for there are, in addition to all that has been said here about the general relationship of these writers, individual virtues and limitations which can be disclosed only by a closer examination of the works themselves.

Of the non-Southern writers, with the exception of Ernest Hemingway, F. Scott Fitzgerald is undoubtedly the most significant writer of short stories. Of his best-known novel *The Great Gatsby*, T. S. Eliot said that it represented the first important step in the American novel since James. His short stories at their best recall the work of James, too, for they are studies in manners reflecting a sensitivity to social distinctions—particularly the differences engendered by extreme wealth—which is as penetrating as that of James. Unfortunately, Fitzgerald's total production of short stories is marred by hack work, necessitated by his own inordinate need for money. He once wrote a story in a single night, "The Camel's Back." "The Popular Girl," written in a week, brought him fifteen hundred dollars. His best work, however, caught not only the irresponsibility of the years following the first war but pointed also to the sources of personal and moral corruption implicit in a society based upon the social and moral prerogatives of wealth.

Fitzgerald's success following the publication of his first novel *This Side of Paradise* in 1920 was spectacular. His prolific talent made it possible for him to follow up his initial success with two novels and three volumes of short stories during the next five years. After 1925 self-doubt and the pace of his early work began to tell. Nine years were to pass between the completion of *The Great Gatsby* and the publication of his next novel *Tender Is the Night* (1934). Likewise, his first three short-story volumes—*Flappers and Philosophers* (1920), *Tales of the Jazz Age* (1922), and *All the Sad Young Men* (1926)—were not followed by another until *Taps at Reveille* appeared in 1935. But it was not only the loss of youthful confidence and energy which accounted for the slowing down of Fitzgerald's career. Changing social conditions following the stock-market crash of 1929 had made his subject matter seem, for the time being at least, less significant. Fitzgerald's "sad young men" of the years of prosperity took on the coloring of an unintentional irony in the sombre light of the depression years. This period also saw his struggle for a more consciously serious attitude toward his craft accompanied by doubts concerning the course his career had run, accompanied, also, by personal and family difficulties which made the expenditure of continuous literary effort almost an impossibility.

He died of a heart attack in December 1940 at the age of forty-four, leaving an unfinished novel *The Last Tycoon* and many uncollected stories, the best of which were edited and published posthumously in 1951.

Among the many stories which he wrote a few stand out as belonging to the best of our time: "May Day," with its complicated and highly successful weaving of related themes; "The Rich Boy," with its social implications which raise it above the character sketch or the case history which it so closely resembles; and "Babylon Revisited," the late testament of the author's own recognition of the kind of life which he had experienced and so skillfully rendered as characteristic of the Jazz Age.

"May Day" is the story of Gordon Sterrett's last few hours

of life, and the events do in a strange way portray Fitzgerald's anxiety about the times he knew so well—prefigure,
even, his own role in them. The day begins with Gordon's
attempt to obtain financial help from his former Yale class-
mate Philip Dean. Dean is a man of inherited wealth; Gordon, the familiar Fitzgerald privileged outsider—the man
whose ironic privilege it was to associate with the world of
wealth in school and club without actually belonging to it.
Gordon's plea is ignored, but his meeting with Philip does
bring him back into the social circle he had known a few
years earlier as an undergraduate. The year is 1919. The
war has ended, soldiers are being discharged, and the whole
crazy era of the 1920's is just beginning. The events of the
story, while centering upon a fraternity party which Gordon attends with Philip at Delmonico's, moves forward on
three related levels: the events of the party itself, during
which Gordon meets his old college girl again and is re-
membered as the lively and carefree undergraduate; the
small odyssey of two discharged soldiers who accidentally
find themselves drinking at the party before going forth to
participate in the destruction of the offices of the socialist
newspaper nearby; and events in the socialist headquarters
before and during the riot. Through these events Fitzgerald
manages to combine all of the jumbled and seemingly ir-
relevant aspects of the era—the dissipation and irresponsibility, the social prejudice, and the idealism. While the
wealthy young Philip Dean and Peter Himmel engage in
a Roman holiday at a Child's restaurant at sunrise, the ideal-
istic young newspaperman is in the hospital with a broken
leg, one of the soldiers lies dead, and Gordon Sterrett is preparing to put a bullet through his head.

Lionel Trilling has spoken of Fitzgerald's sensitivity to
the same distinctions of social manners as Henry James, and

he is, of course, correct. Fitzgerald lacks the complex insight of James as well as his sustained creative power, but their fiction is of the same order. While authors of the Southern group could construct their stories against a background of regional society, Fitzgerald, like James, drew his characters from the world of inherited wealth and sophistication. Like James's Americans abroad in contact with a world deeper and more inscrutable than any they could have known at home, Fitzgerald usually portrays the meeting of Western restlessness and fluidity with the repose of Eastern security and social rigidity. His young men come out of the West, as he himself came from St. Paul, momentarily to astound and captivate, but finally to succumb to the imponderable weight of social restriction. Like Jay Gatsby, they all "believed in the green light, the orgiastic future that year by year receded before [them]." The green light, it will be recalled, is the light at the end of Daisy Buchanan's dock, the light which signaled nearness and promise but which proved to be only the final, tragic delusion.

The young men and young women that Fitzgerald knew best were disinherited and lost, seeming to possess a world for which they were too good but which they had not yet taken the trouble to deserve. That their frantic search for happiness was more innocent and less evil than the glitter which attracted them we learn from the pictures of the rich in such stories as "A Diamond as Big as the Ritz" and "The Rich Boy." But innocence remains innocent only so long as it retains unself-consciousness. Remorse for its consequences exhibits one form of knowledge. There is something pathetic about Gordon Sterrett's suicide only because it was accomplished in self-pity and resulted merely from his coming up against forces with which his naïve early faith in his own talent could no longer cope. In a later story Fitzgerald projected and deepened the defeat by having Charlie Wales of "Babylon Revisited" recognize and acknowledge his irresponsibility, his failure. Such recognition made it possible for him to savor fully the complex and ironic quality of it.

The central action of "Babylon Revisited" relates Charlie's efforts to regain custody of his child Honoria, who had been taken from him at the time of his wife's death. The setting is Paris in the days following the synthetic gaiety of the 1920's. The era had ended for Charlie when he drunkenly locked his pregnant wife out in the snow during a party which had been only typical of many preceding it. The tragic difference this time is that his wife dies as a result of the exposure, and the child is taken from Charlie and awarded to his sister-in-law. Remorsefully, Charlie moves to Prague and fashions a new life. When he returns to Paris to seek possession of Honoria he again, this time accidentally, becomes involved with some of his old friends; and despite his present dislike of the old life—his knowledge that whatever it was at the time it not only could not be regained but it was something he had to escape if possible, not recover—he appears to have succumbed and thus loses, once and for all, the hope of regaining his child.

The pathos in "Babylon Revisited" is deepened and enriched by Charlie Wales's recognition that he is, in part at least, merely reaping the harvest of his earlier years. His failure is both a punishment and an expiation. The sad young Gordon Sterrett of "May Day" has become the doomed young man Charlie Wales—doomed because he still carries the burden of his early irresponsibility, even in the years of maturity and knowledge.

Kay Boyle, who was also a native of St. Paul, has fashioned a career in many respects similar to F. Scott Fitzgerald's but

lacking the extremes either in her personal life or in the
short stories themselves. Born in 1903, she spent much of
her early life in Washington, D. C., and in Cincinnati, and
she has spent most of the years since 1922 in Europe. Thus
Miss Boyle, even more than Fitzgerald, dissociated herself
from her native background. She has written of herself:
"The longer I live and the more I write, the more completely am I convinced that my interest in people and in
writing is of so unnational a character that, for me, the
question of 'roots' in any particular soil or tradition is not
of any moment." Yet she has utilized her own experiences
both in her novels and stories, and as an American in Europe she has been extremely sensitive to national differences.
Also, her concern with political subjects, which has become
more and more frequent since the 1930's, has represented a
testing of political attitudes through the medium of fiction,
much as Fitzgerald and William Faulkner have tested general social attitudes and ideas.

A good example, and also an example of Miss Boyle at
her best, is her short story "The White Horses of Vienna,"
which won the O. Henry Memorial Prize in 1935. The surface events of the story are slight, involving little more than
the visit of a young Jewish doctor to the isolated office of an
Austrian Nazi, to substitute while the Nazi doctor is inca-
pacitated by an injured leg. The Nazi doctor presents a puppet show which betrays his political sympathies at a time
prior to the German-Austrian *Anschluss* and which also portrays his own attitude toward his young medical colleague.
The young Jew betrays his own attitude by relating the
story of the white Lippizaner horses of Vienna. Although
the story is anti-Nazi in theme, the treatment is so far from
being propagandistic that Clifton Fadiman, one of the O.
Henry judges, wrote that he considered the Austrian doctor

"much too heroic for his role." Actually, this character is not heroic at all. He is competent and cocksure. One does not pity him or even feel sympathy for him. Like the white horses of the vanished Austrian royalty, he arouses the admiration of the young Jewish doctor. In speaking of the horses, the young doctor indicates Miss Boyle's attitude toward his Nazi employer: " 'Still royal,' he said, 'without any royalty left to bow their heads to, still shouldering into the arena with spirits a man would give his soul for, bending their knees in homage to the empty, canopied loges where royalty no longer sat!' " This is, in fact, a description of the Nazi doctor, a man of spirit who considers himself elite in a world which has no "leader" to pay homage to. One can admire his skill and his talents, but one is frightened by the sheer power they represent. In contrast, the young Jew is awkward and romantic, not a man to be feared certainly. He is like the clown in the Nazi doctor's puppet show, putting his faith in clouds, not in the realities which the doctor recognizes. But the young Jew is a man to be pitied because he is a human being. He is, as Miss Boyle suggests, "the Chancellor" compared to "der Führer." He may die because he is too full of admiration and trust, and this is impractical; but it is admirable, and his spirit will survive.

Nazism, then, is seen by Miss Boyle as the survival of the elite in a world where it can no longer function except as a show of spirit and force. Her short story is a study in decadence, not heroism, and, except for its political subject matter, it is not too dissimilar from comparable studies by James and Faulkner. There is something to be admired in a past grandeur, the story seems to say, but such admiration must not lead us to mistake the past for the present. An easy romanticism may lead us to make this mistake, with serious political or social consequences. In the case of Miss

Boyle's story, the consequences follow two directions: the easy persecution of one who puts too much faith in pure beauty disassociated from its function, or the arrogance of him who sets himself above others for the practice of pure power without regard for its human aims.

If Miss Boyle, as a displaced American in Europe during the 1930's, was sensitive to the climate of desperate political activity, her situation was only outwardly different from that of her Southern contemporaries. Brought up with memories of a social grandeur destroyed by civil war, such authors seem at times almost obsessed with the need to examine the values of that society in terms of the ever-changing present. It is as though the violent destruction of that society had impressed upon them the transiency of even the most seemingly stable social order. While the lesser talents retreated into sentimental romanticism, where the glories of the past were revived and admired in short stories and novels of the "moonlight-and-magnolia" school, however, the more genuinely talented among them undertook an examination which neither neglected the values of the past nor overlooked its dangers and limitations. Yet, they were not concerned with Southern life alone, but with all life. The life of the South had been highly mannered, conscious of itself to a point bordering on arrogance. The Civil War, despite the specific issues which caused it and which finally brought about the destruction of the Old South, might be seen as the tragic consequence, excessive and, in part at least, unjust, but deserved and in the tradition of human tragedy nonetheless. Its manners and traditions gave it objectivity and made it more available as literary subject matter than the more fluid history of the North. The contrast of its agrarian and aristocratic past with its present of growing mercantilism and uncertain moral values made it not

only an excellent subject for the study of man's imperma-
nence but the subject, also, for his contemplation of human
valor in the face of seemingly insurmountable odds. As William Faulkner has suggested in numerous novels and short
stories, the South carried the seeds of its own destruction
from the beginning. In part, of course, it was slavery, and
if it had not been slavery it probably would have been
something else. But the story of slavery emphasizes that
mixture of benevolence and cruelty, valor and injustice,
which goes to make up the sum of man's existence. All in
all, what Malcolm Cowley has called "the legend of the
South" provides a background for a tragic concept of human life to which the best Southern writers have not been
blind.

Among the best of these writers is Katherine Anne Porter, who was born in Texas in 1894. Miss Porter spent
several years in Mexico and in Europe before she began
publishing her short stories in the late 1920's. Her first published volume was a limited edition of a few stories published under the title *Flowering Judas* in 1930. In 1935 this
book was expanded and was published in a trade edition. A
second volume, entitled *Pale Horse, Pale Rider,* containing
three long stories, appeared in 1939. *The Leaning Tower
and Other Stories,* which contained eight short stories and
the long title story, was published in 1944. Since then, Miss
Porter has been working on a novel, portions of which have
appeared in various magazines; it will be called *No Safe
Harbor.*

Flowering Judas contains some of Miss Porter's most
excellent stories, including the title story, "Maria Concepción," "Magic," "Rope," "That Tree," "The Jilting of
Granny Weatherall," "The Cracked Looking-Glass," and
"Hacienda." The three long stories in *Pale Horse, Pale*

Rider are "Noon Wine," "Old Mortality," and the title story. *The Leaning Tower* includes such excellent stories as "The Circus," "The Old Order," "The Grave," and "The Downward Path to Wisdom."

Miss Porter's output has not been great, yet there is probably no writer of short stories in America who has maintained so consistently high a level. Her subjects are drawn from her own background: life in the South, in Mexico, and in Europe. Her method of writing she calls "working from memory." When certain memories converge and flow together, then, she says, she has a short story. Her attitude toward her material shows clearly the result of her Roman Catholic upbringing, her Southern background, her travels, and her interest in social causes.

Miss Porter's use of her Mexican experiences is indicated in such stories as "Maria Concepción," "That Tree," "Hacienda," and "Flowering Judas." Her Southern background supplies the materials for "Old Mortality," "Magic," "The Jilting of Granny Weatherall," and most of the shorter stories in *The Leaning Tower*. While her early Catholicism is evident in her general attitude toward her subjects, it comes out most explicitly in "The Cracked Looking-Glass," "Flowering Judas," and "That Tree." Her concern with political subjects is most clearly shown in "The Leaning Tower," "Hacienda," and "Flowering Judas."

The singling out of any particular story as Miss Porter's best is particularly difficult because of the general high quality of her work, but "Flowering Judas," "Pale Horse, Pale Rider," and "Old Mortality" are probably her three most popular stories, with "Maria Concepción" following closely. The first three of these are told, characteristically, from the point of view of a Southern girl, the first two set outside the region, the third, a reflection upon the narrator's own relationship to the romantic myths of her own Southern family contrasted with the less romantic reality of the present. "Maria Concepción" is told from the point of view of a Mexican woman who murders her husband's mistress in order to retain his love. While "Flowering Judas" is probably the most consistently sustained of all Miss Porter's works, sustained tonally as well as thematically, "Pale Horse, Pale Rider" is as rich in meaning and as provocative. The method of each is very close to that of Hawthorne, where a background myth (or myths) is introduced to supply an additional level of meaning. In "Flowering Judas"[1] it is the Christian concept of love and redemption, in "Pale Horse, Pale Rider," the legend of Adam, original sin, and the relationship of man to death.

"Pale Horse, Pale Rider" is set in the concluding days of World War I. It is told from the point of view of Miranda, a twenty-four-year-old Southern girl who works as a reporter on a Western paper. She falls in love with Adam Barclay, a second lieutenant from Texas who has completed his training and is awaiting orders for shipment overseas. Events of the story concern their attempts to find sanity amidst the nightmare hysteria of war, attempts which are frustrated completely when Miranda falls ill with influenza. She recovers, but Adam has been infected by her, and when she awakes from delirium, she learns that he has died at his training camp.

The parallel between this story and the Adam and Eve legend is interesting and meaningful and recalls Hawthorne's use of the same legend in "Rappaccini's Daughter." Combined with the Biblical legend, there is also Miranda's childhood fable of the Pale Horseman, the not

[1] For a more complete analysis of "Flowering Judas," see Ray B. West, Jr., and Robert Wooster Stallman, *The Art of Modern Fiction.*

wholly fearful rider who calls to escort her into the land of shades, but to whom she says, "I'm not going with you this time." Miranda's delirium is really a descent into the world of evil which is represented in life by all of the hypocrisies and cruelties of war and wartime. When she returns, it is to discover that Adam, the personification of health and life, has ridden away with the Pale Rider. But it was also a descent into knowledge, "the downward path to wisdom," as she characterized it in another story. Death and evil were facts to be faced and recognized, not to be hidden behind war slogans or the smooth phrases of the patriotic orators. Adam was gone, and he could not be summoned back by an act of will. All that was left was time —"the dead cold light of tomorrow." The war, too, was a descent, and so the theme broadens and picks up the specific incidents concerning the Liberty bond campaign, the visit to the veterans' hospital, and the foolish, impersonal hatred of the foe. Adam's death was, of course, the final descent, and this fact suggests that love, which was the means by which Miranda is saved, was also the first step toward death. The knowledge of this fact is heightened and colored by the irony of Miranda's recovery as well as by the irony of the fact that Adam met death, not on the battlefield, but at a training camp on the very eve of the Armistice.

One of Miss Porter's outstanding technical achievements is the skillful manner in which she introduces her themes through the use of accepted mythical concepts. She is, in this respect, superior even to Hawthorne and Melville, who, for all their superlative qualities, forever seemed concerned that their central themes would be overlooked by their readers. Miss Porter's method is nearer to that of Henry James, where the subject matter—to use a phrase of James's —"bristles with implications," yet where all of the implications can finally be located and understood as well as felt. In only one of her major stories does Miss Porter offend by an overspecification of her symbols, and that is in the long title story of her most recent collection, the story entitled "The Leaning Tower."

Two other Southern writers of short fiction whose skill at its best equals that of Miss Porter are Caroline Gordon and Robert Penn Warren. Neither has equalled Miss Porter's impressive record, but much of the energy of both Miss Gordon and Mr. Warren has gone into the writing of novels, and both must be considered among the best novelists of our generation. Both are natives of the state of Kentucky. Both utilize their Southern background almost exclusively as subject matter for their fiction.

Miss Gordon's best known character is one who provides the subject for what is probably her most admired novel, *Alec Maury, Sportsman.* He also figures in much of her short fiction. Maury is a scholar by profession but a sportsman by inclination. He thus combines in his own person the qualities which other Southern writers like Faulkner and Warren seem to see as the principal qualities of life as a whole. The primitive rituals survive in the acts of the sportsman, for whom the proper lure, the proper fishing or hunting grounds, and the necessary skill represent objects and actions responded to with a passionate intensity, resembling on the one hand our response to art, on the other, our response to nature.

"Old Red"—one of the Alec Maury series—is probably Caroline Gordon's most completely successful short story, although such stories as "Her Quaint Honor," "The Captive," and a very recent one, "The Waterfall," are also among the best of our time. "The Ice-House" and "The Forest of the South"—the latter supplying the title for her single collection of stories—deal with Civil War subjects. Miss Gordon's acknowledged masters are Chekhov and Henry James.

In addition to his volume of short stories, Robert Penn Warren has also published four excellent novels, a collected edition of his poems, and several volumes of criticism. He was for many years at Louisiana State University, where he edited, with Cleanth Brooks, the most highly respected literary journal in America during the 1930's, *The Southern Review*. With Mr. Brooks he was also co-author of two extremely influential literary textbooks: *Understanding Poetry* and *Understanding Fiction*.

As the youngest member of the Fugitive group of poets who were at Vanderbilt University in Nashville in the 1920's and who included among them Donald Davidson, John Crowe Ransom, and Allen Tate, Mr. Warren might almost be said to belong to the most recent generation of American writers. However, most of his short stories come from the period during the 1930's when he was editing *The Southern Review,* even though they were not collected until 1948, by which time he had published his first three novels.

Considering the fact that the bulk of Robert Penn Warren's short stories were among the first of his literary productions, it is not surprising that they are more uneven in quality than most of his other work or than the work of either Miss Porter or Miss Gordon. They range in quality from the sprawling but interesting "The Circus in the Attic" to the almost perfectly controlled "Blackberry Winter." Also, "Blackberry Winter" might be cited as a story which incorporates and combines almost all of the thematic concerns of the Southern group. It is a story of the type which Warren himself has called "the story of initiation," but one which goes further, perhaps, than any other contemporary short story of its kind in defining specifically the nature of the evil which confronts man and with which he must eventually come to some kind of terms. Compared with it, such stories as Ernest Hemingway's "My Old Man" and Faulkner's "That Evening Sun," excellent as they are, seem thin and incomplete. Like them, it is a story told·from the point of view of a child, but told in retrospect to avoid the limitations of the straight childhood narrative.

On its simplest level, "Blackberry Winter" is merely the story of a day in the life of a young Southerner, a day in late spring known as blackberry winter because it is a period of unnatural regression from the warmth and comfort of spring, a day when the customary attitudes of the young boy toward the calendar, toward the authority of his parents, toward his relations with the Negroes of his place, toward mankind in general, must be suddenly and dramatically revised. It is the day, in short, in which the transition from boyhood to manhood, from innocence to knowledge, is accomplished. The story is rich in ironies because the author has utilized a set of dual contrasts in the manner of Faulkner and James. Nature, for instance, is depicted as benevolent, rooted, timeless, represented by the trees which the boy remembers as standing in the stillness of the forest where the static quiet is broken only by the clocklike dripping of the water from the leaves. It is regular and dependable, like the ticking of a watch or the movement of the seasons. Yet nature is evil, too, as now when the blackberry winter intrudes with its unseasonable dampness and cold, its illness and threat of illness, its floods which bring dispossession and even death. Nature is benevolent when it supplies food for the body, but there are times, as one character says, when a man will settle for anything, including "drownt cow." Likewise, humankind is benevolent, as depicted in the persons of the boy's parents, the symbols of authority, rooted and belonging to this place where the boy belongs, certain in their relation to the land and to their neighbors. There are times, however, when human nature goes out of control as the river does during floodtime. At such times even parental love appears as hate, as when the Negro maid, ill in her cabin, strikes her child for an offense which would at another time have been overlooked. There is, above all, the transient stranger who wanders across the land, not searching for the usual employment, not knowing even how to do the usual jobs, but merely seeking a means of getting from one unknown place to another. Compared to the boy's father, whose very clothes suggest his belonging to this place, this occupation, and this time, the tramp is dressed in the remnants of clothes belonging to a man from elsewhere, a city man but not a gentleman, for his shoes are cracked and worn and his other finery faded and anonymous. Even the features and the actions of the tramp, with his pasty complexion and his sneaky way of drawing a knife when the dogs approach him, are characteristics of anonymity—absence of specification, mystery.

The mystery of transiency in man and nature is the subject of the story. It suggests the impossibility of absolute order either in nature or in man. The presence of disorder and the need to accept and deal with it is recognized by the boy. His recognition is portrayed through a fascination with the tramp. "God damn you, you little son of a bitch! Don't you follow me!" the tramp tells him. "But I have," the narrator of the story, who is the boy grown, tells us. "I have followed him all the days of my life."

This is the tragedy of man seen in modern terms. Man's limitations exist in his uncertain relationship with nature.

Nature is timeless; as other centuries, and particularly the nineteenth, came to know. But it is also time itself, and time brings change. Such a story as "Blackberry Winter" should sufficiently refute those readers who have maintained that our traditionalists, particularly the Southern group of writers, wish to retain only the ordered past of their ancestors. Such readers see only one side of the problem. It is true that such writers relinquish traditional values only partially and with reluctance, that they regret the passing of any workable system of values; but they recognize the passing of values as the principal tragic fact of present-day existence, and such recognition is the nearest that any age has ever come to conceiving of an absolute value. As the young man of Robert Penn Warren's short story turns from the almost perfectly regulated life with his parents on the small Southern farm, so the intelligent human being turns necessarily from the deceptive security of the immediate past to the present and the future—to the mysterious dangers of the as-yet-unknown. The uncertainty frightens and challenges him. Such a concept is the lesson which the traditionalist writers of the short story pose against the social optimism of the reformers and the naturalists.

Several other writers of this period must be mentioned, for while their work in the short story is less impressive than that of those authors already considered, they have added color and variety to the accomplishments of these years. Among the Southerners, Ellen Glasgow, a Virginian, built an impressive but quiet reputation as an author of fiction portraying the life of her region. She was, however, primarily a novelist, publishing only a single volume of short stories, *The Shadowy Third* in 1923, compared to twenty novels published between 1897 and 1941. A serious critical examination of her work is long overdue, but it

belongs rightly to the history of the American novel. Her
stories represent a competent, but not too exciting, contribution to Southern writing.

A displaced Southerner, Wilbur Daniel Steele, born in
North Carolina but brought up in Colorado, fashioned a
considerable reputation as a short-story writer in the 1920's.
Writing in the dramatic tradition of Jack London, and
never far from the formula of popular fiction, his stories
went out of style in the 1930's, and Mr. Steele turned to
the writing of plays. At their best, his stories miss genuine
significance primarily because of the rigidity with which he
held the concept of the short story as primarily an adventure, much in the manner of Jack London, but without
London's unconventionality or his vigorous social attitudes.
Reading his stories today, one is still impressed by the bril-
liant surface glitter of them but struck, too, by what seems
finally a false manipulation of material for its dramatic effect. His craftsmanship is sure—almost too predictable. And
it is utilized too much for its own sake. Life gives way before it. As with O. Henry and other masters of this type of
writing, once the trick is seen, too little remains to satisfy
the demanding reader.

An even more spectacular career than Wilbur Daniel
Steele's was fashioned by William Saroyan in the 1930's.
Saroyan's short story "The Daring Young Man on the Fly-
ing Trapeze" was written in 1933 and first published in
Story magazine. As the unconventional portrait of a young
artist starving to death in the midst of American plenty, this
story suggested the possibility of a fresh approach to the
then popular story of social protest. Combined with its
author's talent for self-dramatization and experiment, it
formed the basis for an almost mythical reputation in
which William Saroyan was seen as the brash young Cali-

fornia-Armenian storming the citadel of traditional art, as story after story followed the first—ten volumes between 1934 and 1941, in addition to plays, articles, pronouncements, and a novel which made the best-seller lists in 1943. Saroyan saw his work as introducing "a little freedom into whatever future American expression might seek in the short story form."

Viewing William Saroyan's amazing grab bag of fiction now, however, we realize that he mistook license for freedom. Possessing a genuine talent for freshness of phrase, he produced a few early works which were rightly seen as an impressive beginning for a young author. On the whole, however, his early stories remain his best, and too many of what he considered to be short stories were little more than personal essays and anecdotes. One seeks in vain through his multitudinous production for even a single story which exhibits a genuine awareness of problems which have concerned our major writers from the beginning. One discovers an author with an interesting, if egocentric, personality; one hears glib Shavian pronouncements uttered without irony and with little excuse except self-dramatization; one recognizes the familiar form of the bohemian poseur, altered only slightly by its California accent. And perhaps this is the truth, finally, about William Saroyan.

Yet, at the same time, one regrets the possibility of a talent wasted; for in his native ability and in the materials of his California-Armenian background Saroyan possesses a combination which might have resulted in a significant career as a writer of short stories. His works, however, are less an examination of the colorful and interesting life he knew well than they are a portrait of the author himself. We do not see the Armenian colony of Southern California through his eyes; for the figure of the author, a dull and pretentious young man, gets in our way. Lacking the careful apprenticeship of the genuine writer, he lacks also the techniques for dealing with his material. His own shadow blots out the light and destroys the focus of his work. Now that we can no longer think of William Saroyan as a promising, if pretentious, young writer, we have lost all excuse for taking his work seriously, even as an experiment in American fiction.

More difficult to assess, because quieter and more sincere, are the experimental short stories of Conrad Aiken and William Carlos Williams. Both of these authors are primarily poets, and both write in a prose as clean and controlled as William Saroyan's is cluttered. Both have been influenced by modern science, Conrad Aiken by the theories of psychoanalysis, in which he has taken a great personal interest, and William Carlos Williams by modern medical science, in which field he is an active practitioner. Conrad Aiken's best work, such a story as "Silent Snow, Secret Snow," resembles the stories of James Joyce's *Dubliners* in its use of psychological symbols and a quiet penetration into themes underlying its outward events. Compared with Joyce, or even with such American authors as Katherine Anne Porter or Robert Penn Warren at their best, however, his work approaches, but lacks, the final concentration and completeness to rank him among the outstanding writers of the age. Dr. Williams's stories, on the other hand, are almost willfully incomplete. Individual stories are conceived as parts of a whole, rather than as completed forms, so that whatever completeness they have is achieved in relation to each other, not within themselves. The author's method is that of the surgeon—as suggested in the title of Williams's best-known collection *The Knife of the Times, and Other Stories* (1932)—in which the corpus of society is laid open by the scalpel and examined part by part. In a few stories, such as his most popular story "The Use of Force," a controlling idea supplies a measure of form which raises the individual work out of its general dependence upon other stories. On the whole, however, his separate works are less short stories than they are brief, incisive character sketches or personal anecdotes; and the final form, coming as it does from the total volume, seems nearer to the form of the novel than it does to that of short fiction. No single story achieves the interest or importance of the total work.

Nevertheless, all of these authors added excitement and importance to the development of the short story during the 1920's and 1930's. They assisted in the creation of a period which, to the present at least, surpasses any comparable period in the history of the American short story. The crowning achievement of these years, however, is represented in the work of two authors who excelled not only in the quality of individual stories which they contributed to a growing list of important works by Americans in this form, but whose total production represents an astonishing and consistently high level of creative activity; so much so that a separate chapter must be devoted to their work.

HEMINGWAY AND FAULKNER
Two Masters of the
Modern Short Story

I T SEEMS clear that the two most significant American writers of fiction in the first half of the twentieth century are Ernest Hemingway and William Faulkner. Whether their reputations are based primarily upon their novels or upon their short stories is not important. Undoubtedly their popular reputations are based upon their novels. Critics have persisted, however, in calling attention to the excellence of their short stories. In fact, it is probably in the realm of the short story that the supremacy of these two authors is least in question. Their art, interesting and important as it always is, falters occasionally in even the best of their novels—and the best (such works as *A Farewell to Arms* and *The Sound and the Fury*) come nearer to being extended short stories than they do to approaching the limits of the novel form. The best of their stories stand comparison with the finest works of all time, with the stories of Chekhov, Maupassant, Balzac, Flaubert, and Joyce in Europe; with the works of Hawthorne, Melville, Poe, and James in America.

Both authors are wholly the product of the twentieth century. Ernest Hemingway was born in Illinois in 1898, and he published his first collection of short stories in 1924. William Faulkner was born in Mississippi in 1897, and his first short stories appeared in magazines in 1930, in book form in 1931. Since the summer of 1950, when the *Collected Stories of William Faulkner* appeared, the total output of both authors has been readily available. Ernest Hemingway's *The Fifth Column and the First Forty-Nine Stories* has been in print since 1938, and it has since been reissued in a popular edition as *The Short Stories of Ernest Hemingway.*

ii

Ernest Hemingway's first volume of short stories *In Our Time* contained such well-known stories as "Indian Camp," "The Doctor and the Doctor's Wife," "The End of Something," "Soldier's Home," "Mr. and Mrs. Elliot," "Cross-Country Snow," "My Old Man," and "Big, Two-Hearted River." His second volume *Men Without Women* appeared in 1927, and included in it were stories such as "The Undefeated," "In Another Country," "Hills Like White Elephants," "The Killers," and "Fifty Grand." *Winner Take Nothing* appeared in 1933 and included such stories as "A Clean, Well-Lighted Place," "Wine of Wyoming," and "The Gambler, The Nun, and The Radio." *The Short*

Stories mentioned above added four previously unpublished stories, at least three of them among Hemingway's best: "The Short Happy Life of Francis Macomber," "The Capital of the World," and "The Snows of Kilimanjaro."

William Faulkner's first volume *These Thirteen* contained such stories as "Victory," "Ad Astra," "All the Dead Pilots," "Red Leaves," "A Rose for Emily," "A Justice," and "That Evening Sun." His second volume *Doctor Martino, and Other Stories* was published in 1934 and included "Doctor Martino," "The Hound," "Smoke," "Wash," "Elly," "Mountain Victory," and "Honor." From this point on until the publication of *Collected Stories* in 1950 it is difficult to say which of the published collections Faulkner considered to be, strictly speaking, short stories at all, since such volumes as *The Unvanquished* (1938), *Go Down, Moses, and Other Stories* (1942), and *Knight's Gambit* (1949), while they contained stories often published separately in magazines and anthologies, possess a loose kind of unity in their totality, and since selections from them were not included in the *Collected Stories*.

As a matter of fact, the problem is more complicated than this even, since Faulkner often published excerpts from his novels as short stories. Sometimes such excerpts were rewritten, sometimes not. My own belief is that the fact that Faulkner did not include a previously published short story in *Collected Stories* does not necessarily mean that he did not consider it to be a short story; rather, that since the particular ordering of stories in the collected edition was obviously designed to fill in the mythical background of his legendary Yoknapatawpha County, he included only stories from those volumes which did not contain such an ordering or stories which had not previously had book publication.

Certainly, however, it would be a great mistake not to consider such a story as "Spotted Horses," which appears

as a section in *The Hamlet* (1940), as a short story simply because it appears elsewhere as an integrated part of a
novel. There would be even less reason for so considering
such pieces as "Ambuscade" and "Raid" from *The Unvanquished* or "Pantaloon in Black," "Delta Autumn," "Gold
Is Not Always," and "The Bear" from *Go Down, Moses*.
Stories included in *Collected Stories,* not previously printed
in book form, include "The Tall Men," "Mule in the
Yard," "A Courtship," "Lo," "My Grandmother Millard,"
and "Golden Land."

In any general discussion of the work of Ernest Hemingway it has become a commonplace to refer to evidence from
his novels which seem to indicate a gradual shifting from a
philosophy of despair in *The Sun Also Rises* and *A Farewell to Arms* to an attitude of social and moral acceptance
beginning in *To Have and Have Not* and culminating in
For Whom the Bell Tolls and *Across the River and into
the Trees*. Such a development is less obvious in the short
stories, and indeed the short stories have been the starting
point, if not the basis, for whatever qualification has been
made of such a theory. It is true that the short stories of *In
Our Time* present a series of portrayals in the same somber
mood as that depicted in the early novels, portray a world
of lost values and lost illusions; yet, we have come to recognize that underlying such a world there existed for Hemingway an orderly if shrunken universe of recognizable
value. Though the abstract ideals of justice, honor, and pa-
triotism are lost forever, the concrete realization of what
these abstractions are meant to stand for exists eternally
in the natural universe. It exists in the simple sensation
of fishing or hunting; in the common pleasures of eating,
drinking, and sleeping; in the admirable exercise of one's
physical prowess and skill in warfare, the boxing ring, or

the bullfight; in all of those activities where one acquires the ability to live with a knowledge of pain and death. Such a world becomes increasingly visible in such stories as "The Undefeated" and "The Killers" from *Men Without Women,* "The Capital of the World" and "The Short Happy Life of Francis Macomber" from *The Short Stories,* and it becomes finally overstated and sentimentalized in "The Snows of Kilimanjaro" from the same book.

Parallels have been drawn between Hemingway's early work and *The Waste Land* of T. S. Eliot, and certainly there is a resemblance, if only a superficial one. While Eliot sets the sterility of modern life against a rich background of historic and religious myth, Hemingway contrasts the emptiness of ordinary living with the heightened and ritualized activity of warfare and the sports-ring. Actually, however, the parallels (for whatever they are worth) seem closer in the case of Faulkner and Eliot, for William Faulkner's eclectic and disintegrating present, the world of carpetbaggers and Snopeses, stands in meaningful contrast to both the ambiguous innocence of primitive Indian life and the rich decay of Southern aristocratic society.

Since Faulkner seems most consciously intent upon weaving his total work into an elaborate mosaic to portray the history of his mythical county in Mississippi, neither the stories nor the novels alone present the complete background chronicle. Yet each separate work draws upon it for an energy and an additional level of meaning without being dependent upon a full understanding or recognition of it for its essential unity as an independent story or novel. Here it is, perhaps, that both Faulkner and Hemingway (but Faulkner in particular) appear to be widening the bounds of our modern concept of the short story, perhaps even to do violence to our understanding of the modern story as a self-contained literary work. The fact remains, however, that though the background materials add another significant level to the total body of work by each author, the best of the short stories depend very little upon it. Or, to put it another way, where they do depend upon it, such material is supplied within the story itself.

All literature makes an appeal to commonly held values, usually values which have come into existence as exigencies of community living and which are held in common by most members of society. For an author to make such an appeal is not ordinarily considered a breach of unity in his work, since the appeal is no more than that made in all art —the appeal of the object within a work of art as a symbol of the life which it is intended to represent. The world of values is truly a part of the living world of human activity which it is the artist's aim to depict in his art. Thus, Hawthorne made such an appeal when he had much of his fiction deal with a world governed by standards of New England puritan culture. Mark Twain created his most satisfying comic effects by juxtaposing a stern New England morality against the freer, more pragmatic attitudes of frontier society. Henry James, in creating a fiction in which the opposing concepts of Old World culture and the new American liberalism came into close contact, was appealing directly to our common understanding of the cultural differences represented by Europe and America.

There is a sense, however, in which the modern writer of fiction may be said to have created his own somewhat special background of myth and value. Community belief operates less effectively today than it has in the past, and Ernest Hemingway's appeal to the world of war and sport, William Faulkner's continual reference to a mythical Southern past, serve as over-all metaphors to bring about a re-

juvenation of old values in terms which will strike the
modern reader as immediate, fresh, and related to his own
complex needs.

In these terms, we might say that a story such as Hemingway's "The Undefeated" presumes a knowledge of right
conduct in the face of physical danger and possible death.
Within this generality of belief, however, there exists a separate code governing the specific behavior of the bull ring.
Our awareness of these concepts governs our reaction to the
events of the story and the judgment we make concerning
the actions of the characters. Thus, we begin by fearing the
attempts of Manuel Garcia to obtain employment as a bull
fighter. He is too old. He has been inactive too long. Indeed,
as the story progresses, he does fail according to our understanding of the particular kind of performance which the
successful matador is expected to provide. The spectators
show their disapproval by showering him with cushions,
one of which ironically causes him to receive the injury
which (it is implied) may result in death. Yet there is an
important sense—a sense which we understand because of
our general knowledge of how a brave man acts in the face
of danger and defeat—in which Manuel is not defeated. Despite his age and his loss of skill, he retains the courage and
bravery which we recognize as the mark of a successful—an
undefeated—man.

This level of the story does not, of course, represent the
story itself. There are more concrete and more subtle events
which raise the whole action to a plane where it may be
thought to be an imitation of life itself, containing the complexity and richness of life, but it is upon this level that
the principal meaning of the story resides. There are, likewise, other levels—level upon level of meaning, penetrating
to the heart of the action, all relating to this central mean-

ing, organizing and controlling the materials in such a way that they will contribute to the enrichment of the central theme. All are disclosed in the same manner: by referring to a common body of belief, by presenting the materials in such a manner that we may, consciously or unconsciously, recognize not only the principal intentions, but all of the minor, contributing intentions of the work as well.

It has been suggested that modern art, in particular, has grown out of a dissatisfaction with existing belief. Ernest Hemingway has been seen as a rebel against those standards of conduct which generations before World War I appeared to accept as adequate and perfectly satisfactory. There is a sense, however, in which this represents the condition of all art. To put it another way, each artist recognizes the impossibility of his age, or any age, achieving any final or absolute knowledge of truth. Nineteenth-century romanticism in England and in America, particularly during the latter half of the age, was relatively complacent; but complacency became an impossibility following the shock of war. The questions the artists seemed to be asking were: "What values of the past are illusory? Which have value for us today? In what terms do they have value? Are there new values more suitable to the present, and are they also illusory or are they vitally related to our needs?"

These and similar questions seem to lie behind the artistry of both Hemingway and Faulkner. In particular, William Faulkner chooses the changing social conditions of the South following the Civil War as a setting for a body of fiction which is never far from a preoccupation with the meaning of change in terms of the static—and absolute—social structure of the past. In such a story as "A Rose for Emily,"[1]

1 For a more complete analysis of this story, see Ray B. West, Jr., and Robert Wooster Stallman, *The Art of Modern Fiction.*

this concept is mirrored, first of all, in the very description of the setting in which the action takes place. Emily's old house is seen as the impervious but dated family mansion, standing in obsolete ugliness, surrounded by garages and cotton gins, wagons and gasoline pumps. A house which must have seemed an architectural triumph in its own day has now become a symbol not only of the certainty of decay but, in its relationship to the machinery of modern life, a symbol also of the relationship of past and present. It is in these terms, too, that Miss Emily herself is portrayed, first, in her own day as a slender figure in white, silhouetted against the door with her stern and uncompromising father, then, as a pathetic and colorless figure teaching china painting to a generation of children, finally, as a frustrated mistress of a Yankee laborer, retreating into the shadowy past of her old mansion, attempting, almost by force of will alone, to halt the natural process of decay and death, to preserve a love which never existed.

This subject is more complex than the subject of Hemingway's "The Undefeated," the concept of its underlying myth less easy to draw upon. Nevertheless, it is a difference of degree only, for the significant discoveries are made through the particularities of action and scene, not in a mere recognition of the total, over-all view. Hemingway's most characteristic method of establishing atmosphere—of communicating his attitude toward his materials—is by the use of a style which presents the action of war, of the hunt, the prize fight, and the bull ring with an almost ritualistic intensity of detail, thus suggesting that such activities are to be taken with a seriousness almost equal to that of religious ceremony; that is, he concentrates our attention upon isolated details until we see them as symbols of ethical significance. Faulkner, on the other hand, employs a variety of stylistic devices, varying from the suggestive and rich description of an object to the weighted and complicated discourse of an "intelligence" centered in one of his characters. Faulkner's effect is often gained by the coupling or juxtaposing of unusual words, words often so unfamiliar in context that they force an exceptional concentration and examination before yielding up their meaning. Thus, when we read that Miss Emily's house was left, "lifting its *stubborn* and *coquettish* decay above the cotton wagons and the gasoline pumps," the two personifying adjectives make us aware of the horribly grotesque nature of the subject. They also prepare us for a more explicit statement concerning the subject, which is not a concern merely with old houses but with the quality of their oldness. As the unnamed narrator of Faulkner's story tells us, Miss Emily and the old Confederate soldiers confuse "time with its mathematical progression, as the old do, to whom all the past is not a diminishing road but, instead, a huge meadow which no winter ever quite touches, divided from them now by the narrow bottle-neck of the most recent decade of years." Emily's house was like an old harlot, stubbornly and coquettishly (but also grotesquely) denying the passage of time. It was like Emily, denying the death of her father and of Homer Barron, until trapped finally by the fact of her own. In addition, Emily's tragedy was by extension the tragedy of that segment of Southern society which worships its past and denies the existence of its present. By further extension, it is the tragedy of mankind, Southern and Northern, American or European, confronted by the necessity to select and honor that of the past which is applicable and helpful, to recognize and accept that of the present which is beneficial or which cannot be escaped.

The differences in method between Ernest Hemingway

and William Faulkner consist primarily in Hemingway's intense concentration upon those activities which have developed formal means of dealing with life at its most active moments and in Faulkner's examination of life in the present in terms of social and religious forms which he finds existing in his Southern past. The method of each implies a complementary, if not equal, value to be found both in the forms of the past and in the actions of the present. Each is concerned with breaking down and examining the forms which they draw upon. However, neither author is satisfied merely to illustrate the simple truth or falsity of them. Each sees his subject as complex and multiform, so that the stories become an embodiment of the final theme, or idea (which is never quite the same as the underlying myth), existing only as the idea exists within it. The stories do not exist as actions, paralleling and illustrating preconceived attitudes and ideas.

Within the body of the work of each of these authors there is, however, a division into two more or less separate types of short story, practiced more or less equally by each, as each is practiced more or less equally to most contemporary writers of the short story. The first type is of the kind described above, the completed action in which the myth is introduced, examined in terms of a present action, its ambiguities disclosed, even, occasionally, resolved. Of this type we would consider Hemingway's "The Capital of the World" and, insofar as it succeeds, "The Snows of Kilimanjaro"; Faulkner's "The Tall Men," "Turnabout" (a much underrated story, and one in which Faulkner's method comes closest to Hemingway's), and many others. The second type, sometimes called "the story of initiation" or "the story of recognition," is one in which the problem is presented, usually through the consciousness of a central character, in all its distracting and confusing complexity. This kind of story usually portrays the progress of a character from innocence to knowledge. In theological terms, that knowledge is a knowledge and a recognition of evil. To adopt a more secular term we might say, however, that it represents a knowledge of the limitations of existence—the limitations of both nature (the present) and the myth (the past).

This second type has been a favorite with American authors. One reason for its appeal, I think we can assume, is that it can be stated in terms suggestive of the principal philosophical dilemma of our time. Merely by making use of the conventional phrase, "the American tradition," we can, I think, suggest the dilemma, since the very tradition to which we refer represents a rebellion against tradition, a rebellion particularly against the forms of European culture, but also a rebellion against any form which tends to become excessively restrictive or fixed—as forms inevitably tend to become. The rejection of a particular form is certainly desirable if the form has come to function primarily in its own interest—that is, as a means of preserving itself, not as an adequate method of government or as a means of achieving social justice. The dilemma of all who retain even the slightest respect for form results from the tendency of a highly formal society to perpetuate customs and manners which have little or no relationship to life in the present, as opposed to the tendency of an overliberal society to deny all formal social or political structure. These are the extremes which Henry James used in his fiction: the myth of European decadence contrasted with our concept of the vigorous but innocent utilitarianism of the New World.

The story of initiation makes direct use of the dilemma. It suggests that the ordinary means of dealing with the prob-

lems of existence are, first, to recognize that there is a problem, second, to understand that the problem is capable
of only a limited solution. It assumes that a primary step
in the achievement of knowledge is the recognition that
though human justice is desirable, it is not immediately
attainable. It assumes, further, that an important stage in
the process of self-understanding has been achieved when
one learns to live with knowledge. Such is the initiation
which all must undergo. The exact terms in which the discovery occurs, however, is the subject matter of the story—
the subject matter of such stories as Hemingway's "My Old
Man," "The Killers," and "A Clean, Well-Lighted Place,"
or of Faulkner's "That Evening Sun."

The particular subject matter of Hemingway's short story
"A Clean, Well-Lighted Place" is the discovery that traditional religious forms no longer serve to define man's place
in the modern world: "It was all a nothing and a man was
nothing too." The most one can do is to seek the comfort
and dignity of "a clean, well-lighted place." In a savage par-
ody of the Lord's Prayer, which defines the theological frame
of reference for the story, the emptiness and futility of modern life is set off against the traditional expressions of hu-
mility and belief: "Our nada who art in nada, nada be thy
name thy kingdom nada thy will be nada in nada as it is in
nada. . . ." The "discovery" in this story is a reader's recognition, his discovery of the pathetic need of mankind for even
the most limited kind of security and order. The characters
are a barman, a waiter, and an old man, none of them possessing the dignity even of names. Some critics have maintained that the subject of this story is "nada"—nothing.[2] But
it is also the story of modern man's search for dignity amidst
the destruction of old values. The pathos is occasioned by

[2] See particularly Mark Schorer, *The Story: A Critical Anthology.*

our recognition of the extremely limited nature of the relief as set against an implicit lost plenitude.

The discovery in "My Old Man" and "The Killers"[3] is shared by the principal characters. The boy, Joe, of the first story, is forced to recognize the truth about his father, which is that though he was "one swell guy," he was also a crook and a cheat. Nick Adams, in "The Killers," faces the final fact of the irrationality of death, and thus of evil, in his being confronted with the facts of Ole Andreson and his relationship with the world of "the killers." At the same time, it is a realization by the reader of the means for dealing with such knowledge as is represented in the characters of Ole, who is doomed to death for a violation of the code of gangsterdom; Sam, who refuses even to acknowledge the existence of such a world; and George, who has learned to accept and live with his knowledge.

Faulkner's "That Evening Sun" is similar in that it displays the exposure of the three children of Jason Compson to the state of terror inhabited by their Negro maid, Nancy, whose wanton living midway between the worlds of whites and blacks has left her unprotected by the code of either, susceptible both to the lawful fury of Mr. Stovall and to the animal-like fury of her Negro lover. The discovery is complicated, as it is in "The Killers," by the fact that each of the principal characters makes his own adjustment to the facts. The boy Jason, in "That Evening Sun," assumes that because he is "not a nigger," he is protected from Nancy's terror. Caddy Compson, like Nick Adams of "The Killers," is intrigued by the nature of evil itself; while Quentin (who is the narrator of the story, and through whose eyes the in-

3 For an extended analysis of this story, see Cleanth Brooks and Robert Penn Warren, *Understanding Fiction* (New York, Appleton-Century-Crofts, 1943).

cidents are seen) seems to have recognized that the knowledge of evil is a permanent condition of human life.

Not all stories divide themselves easily into these two
types. There is another—perhaps even a higher—kind of
story which appears to combine the elements of both. In
such a story the initiation occurs, but it occurs primarily
as a preparation for a series of actions which display the
effects of such knowledge upon the human character. As
such, it defines in modern terms the specific conditions (usually tragic) under which it is possible for the modern hero
to live with the conflicting knowledge of man's nobility *and*
his meanness. If it is a higher form of story than those already discussed, it is higher than the first because the first
type of story must make its appeal primarily in terms of
traditional values, or values already more or less fixed in
the reader's consciousness; it is higher than the second because the second type, such as "The Killers" or "That Evening Sun," deals primarily with definition, with the conditions under which human tragedy is to be enacted, not with
the tragedy itself. As examples of this type I would suggest
such stories as Hemingway's "The Short Happy Life of
Francis Macomber" and Faulkner's "The Bear."

Perhaps it is wrong to cite such stories as examples of a
type. In structure they are similar to "The Undefeated"
and "A Rose for Emily." They are similar, however, primarily in that they exhibit a completed, rather than a
continuing, action. They differ only insofar as "The Short
Happy Life" and "The Bear" create, at least in part, the
background myth against which the events are enacted.
They pick up and incorporate the ritual of initiation, which
in "The Killers" and "That Evening Sun" represents the
whole of the action, and they use it primarily to define the
terms in which the larger, more all-encompassing action

takes place. They are more completely satisfying, not only because they are more contemporary in the specification of their subject matter, but also because the mythical background is objectified and concretized by reference to events in the story, not made to depend so completely upon abstract concepts such as "honor," "pride," "decorum," etc. In short, they are both *more contemporary* and *more completely realized*.

Briefly, "The Short Happy Life"[4] deals with man's behavior when confronted, at moments of crisis, with the problems of sexual relations in modern marriage, physical terror, and death. More specifically, it deals with the result of that knowledge upon the actions of Francis Macomber, an American sportsman engaged both in discovering a basis for living with his wife and in facing up to the physical danger represented by the events of a big-game hunt. Macomber's discovery is a recognition of the sterile basis of his marriage, forced upon him by a recognition of his own cowardice and of his wife's infidelity. It is not until he has faced these facts honestly that he is capable of willfully pitting his own courage against the animal courage of the water buffalo. The discovery—or initiation—is made in terms of modern (particularly, American) marriage. It represents an examination of the terms of much modern living, reflected in the lives of Francis and Margot Macomber, as well as an examination of the traditional concepts of marital fidelity. The resolution, ironic, even ambiguous, is the resolution presented in all tragedy but provided in terms of modern man's conflict between purely utilitarian and materialistic values and the traditional values of courage, fidelity, and honor.

4 For an extended analysis of this story, see Ray B. West, Jr., and Robert Wooster Stallman, *The Art of Modern Fiction.*

In such general terms, "The Short Happy Life" is little different from Faulkner's important and interesting story, "The Bear." The differences in method, however, between the two stories are both illuminating and provocative. If we are attracted by the riches enclosed and contained by the relatively simple structure of Hemingway's story—the richness of specification and implication, we may well be puzzled, as many readers have been, by the complex scaffolding employed by Faulkner to deal with similar themes.

The pitting of man against the animal has its roots deep within our mythological past. In our own time it has taken on added significance because of its particular aptness to a situation in which nature has become more and more dominant while the stature of man as something outside of nature has shrunk to an apparent insignificance. Thus, the figure of the animal contains not only its original metaphorical designation as an image for man's human limitations, but it has become also ironically symbolic of modern man's predicament as a highly cultivated, abstract, and sterile figure; that is, it has become an aptly ambiguous image, reflecting in two directions. It reveals both the degree of humanity which man has lost by his separation from nature and the degree of human isolation achieved through a purely materialistic concept of man as minute atom in the material universe.

The action of Faulkner's story centers about the hunt for a particularly durable and malignant bear, an animal which, through its very durability and malevolence, has earned itself a name—"old Ben." The specific details of the hunt, which are disclosed over a period of several years in the story, are viewed through the eyes of a young Southerner, Isaac McCaslin, grandson of Carrothers McCaslin, one of the original settlers of Faulkner's mythical Southern county. Isaac is introduced to the wilderness by his cousin, Cass Edmonds; Major de Spain, owner of the land where the hunt takes place; General Compson, Civil War veteran and the son of a former governor of the state; Sam Fathers, whose Indian father conceived him by raping a Negro slave; and Boon Hogganbeck, "in whom some of the same blood ran which ran in Sam Fathers, even though Boon's was a plebeian strain of it": aristocrats and landowners, on the one hand; the dispossessed and deracinated, on the other. Major de Spain is an aristocrat, however, primarily in the sense that he owns the property by law; in another and, Faulkner implies, more real sense, Sam Fathers, the son of an Indian chief and a Negro slave, shares possession of the land with old Ben. He, like the bear, is *of* the land and at the same time master of it by virtue of his skill and knowledge. So far as young Ike, Cass Edmonds, General Compson, and Major de Spain possess that skill and knowledge, they too are rightful possessors of the land. When man becomes, like Boon or like Lion (the mongrel dog which Sam Fathers and Boon train to hunt the bear), simple, malignant animal power, he does not possess, he merely rapes; he becomes a creature of greed and power.

Events of the story are divided into five sections. The first deals with young Ike's introduction to the wilderness and ends with his first sight of the bear, whom he couldn't see (though old Ben had seen him) until he had discarded watch, gun, and compass (the metal, mechanical guides, symbols of man's mastery as well as of his dependence and fear) and delivered himself up to nature itself. The second section opens with Ike's ritualistic baptism by Sam Fathers in the blood of Ike's first buck, and it concerns itself principally with the capture and training of Lion, the powerful mongrel with whose help the hunters draw the first blood from old Ben. Section three contains the successful hunt in which the bear is cornered and killed by Lion and Boon, the dog catching the bear by the throat, the man clinging to his back and stabbing him with powerful strokes, more telling than the blasts of the gun which he could never master. (It is significant to our definitions above that these sections were published separately in magazines in 1934 and 1935 as separate stories entitled "Lion" and "The Bear Hunt." The former is obviously a story of initiation when read out of its larger context.) The death of the bear means the death of old Sam Fathers too, not so much because of the exertion and exposure of the hunt, as because following the death of old Ben—the passing of the wilderness—"he just quit." Section four represents a kind of litany in which Isaac McCaslin relates his reasons for relinquishing his rights to the land bequeathed him by his fathers; for, as he explains to his cousin Cass:

I cant repudiate it. It was never mine to repudiate. It was never Father's and Uncle Buddy's to bequeath to me to repudiate because it was never Grandfather's to bequeath them to bequeath me to repudiate because it was never old Ikkemotubbe's to sell to Grandfather for bequeathment and repudiation. Because it was never Ikkemotubbe's fathers' fathers' to bequeath Ikkemotubbe to sell to Grandfather or any man because on the instant when Ikkemotubbe discovered, realized, that he could sell it for money, on that instant it ceased ever to have been his forever, father to father to father, and the man who bought it bought nothing. (Pp. 256–57)[5]

This section recounts the evil prefigured in the history of the McCaslin-Edmonds property, much of it suggested in excerpts from the commissary accounts to which Ike refers

[5] Page references to quotations refer to *Go Down, Moses, and Other Stories*, original edition (New York, Random House, 1942).

as he speaks: the buying of the land from Ikkemotubbe, the Chickasaw chief; the assembling of slaves, including Tomasina, the mother of the half-breed descendants of Ike's grandfather, Carrothers; the death of Tomy (as she was called) by self-drowning because she felt disgraced; the willing of $1,000 to the son, Tomy's Turl (Terrel), in attempted expiation; the family background and the national background, until:

The boy himself had inherited it as Noah's grandchildren had inherited the Flood although they had not been there to see the deluge: that dark corrupt and bloody time while three separate peoples had tried to adjust not only to one another but to the new land which they had created and inherited too and must live in for the reason that those who had lost it were no less free to quit it than those who had gained it were:—those upon whom freedom and equality had been dumped overnight and without warning or preparation or any training in how to employ it or even just endure it and who misused it not as children would nor yet because they had been so long in bondage and then so suddenly freed, but misused it as human beings always misuse freedom, so that he thought *Apparently there is a wisdom beyond even that learned through suffering necessary for a man to distinguish between liberty and license.* (Pp. 289–90)

These are the terms in which Isaac McCaslin has come to see not only the problems of the South but the problems of human existence as mirrored in the South. Most specifically, however, they are the problems of our time—the growth of greed and power from the pastoral-primitive Indian days through the agrarian slave society preceding the Civil War and into the mercantile rapacity not only of reconstruction but of the modern world. Section five applies these attitudes in terms of the final events of the story. Isaac McCaslin returns to the wilderness as it is being destroyed on the one hand by the lumber company which has moved in and begun to cut the timber and on the other hand by the lone survivor, Boon, or by the attitudes he represents, an attitude not too dissimilar to that of the lumbermen—Southern industry, the mongrel breed, just as Boon and Lion are mongrels. Boon is discovered by Ike in the last scene, his back against a tree in which he has cornered an unbelievable number of squirrels; he is frantically hammering at the dismembered and useless gun in his lap, furiously shouting: "Get out of here! Dont touch them! Dont touch a one of them! They're mine!"

Behind Ike, the mechanical efficiency of the industrial world; before him, the barbaric inefficiency of Boon. Both filled with the same furious greed. But greed and power are not enough. Survival demands skill and endurance, and neither the lumber company nor Boon has enough of either to outlast nature. This is perhaps as near as we can come to summarizing the complex theme which William Faulkner has bodied forth in this, one of the most noteworthy achievements of the twentieth-century short story.

However, it is not solely on the basis of individual achievement that we value the short stories of Ernest Hemingway and William Faulkner. Though we may hold it as a personal opinion that "The Short Happy Life of Francis Macomber" and "The Bear" are the two finest examples of the modern short story, we should find it difficult to prove that they were more effective as short stories than, say, Katherine Anne Porter's "Flowering Judas" or Robert Penn Warren's "Blackberry Winter." The final value of Hemingway and Faulkner exists, it is true, in terms of the excellence of their finest stories; but it exists also as an extension of that excellence, in the impressive total body of their work—a total which perhaps can be matched only by Henry

James among short-story writers in America since Hawthorne. Such value exists also in the position of these men as innovators—in those qualities which mark them as not only different but superior to a generation which preceded them. The twentieth century called for revaluation, for a re-examination of the moral and aesthetic principles upon which both American life and American art had been established. Ernest Hemingway and William Faulkner, each in his own way, represent the vanguard of such revaluation in American fiction; and, different though they may seem in many ways, their similarities outweigh the differences. If it becomes increasingly difficult to see them as experimenters—as the *avant-garde,* it is above all because their values have become accepted and incorporated into the tradition. They are not so much revolutionaries as they are counter-revolutionaries. They did not so much deny existing values as they insisted upon a thorough re-examination of them, a re-examination in terms of the life of their times. In the great tradition of literature this is the mark of the genuine artist. Because in their generation and in their media they were the first to see the need and to fulfill it, they justify the title "masters" of the modern short story.

THE SHORT STORY
IN THE FORTIES

WHETHER our short-story writers of the 1940's will prove themselves as successful as their predecessors of the 1920's and the 1930's cannot, of course, be said yet with any real certainty. Their careers are incomplete. One thing does seem clear, however: the most talented among them are continuing in the tradition which leads from Hawthorne and Melville through Henry James to Ernest Hemingway and William Faulkner. Their reality is not the "natural facts" of naturalism so much as it is the complex of beliefs, hopes, and fears which seem, somehow, to motivate the actions of human beings—what William Faulkner, in his speech accepting the Nobel Prize, called "the problems of the human heart in conflict with itself which alone can make good writing because only that is worth writing about, worth the agony and the sweat."

Merely to possess such attitudes does not, however, guarantee the production of great short stories. Talent must accompany knowledge, and true technical proficiency is empty without it. It has been fashionable recently to say of our younger writers that, while they display exceptional ability and knowledge, their work lacks the true excitement of great art. One must be cautious in taking such a statement as final. The history of literature is full of the mistakes made by critics in judging their contemporaries. One should also examine more closely so inconsistent and general a statement. "Exciting for whom?" we might ask. It is always possible that our own ignorance may blind us, make us incapable of feeling an excitement which later readers will sense at once. Yet there is also the possibility that what such critics mean is, merely, that the tools of the craft have come to dominate the works to such an extent that, while we recognize and approve the craftsmanship, we cannot get beyond it and into a feeling for the work itself. Or they might mean that our younger writers seem most intent upon exploiting the techniques and the forms of their predecessors, incapable of fashioning their own. These critics might be saying only what Emerson said over a century ago, that "each age . . . must write its own books; or rather, each generation for the next succeeding. The books of an older period will not fit this."

Here again, however, we must beware of accepting such views without a good deal of evidence. Most recently signs have appeared which indicate a radical revision of opinion. Herschel Brickell, the editor of the annual O. Henry Memorial prize short stories, has recently stated that in his view the short story today "is in a highly flourishing condition artistically."[1] He accounts for this by saying that young

[1] Introduction to *Prize Stories of 1951: The O. Henry Awards* (Garden City, Doubleday, 1951).

THE SHORT STORY IN THE FORTIES

writers take their work more seriously, have a better fundamental understanding of their problems, and are assisted
by a higher quality of editorial judgment than ever before.
Martha Foley, who also edits an annual anthology of short
stories *The Best American Short Stories,* seems equally optimistic. The present generation of short-story writers, she
says, has left the disillusion of the 1920's far behind: "A
generation that has known both a terrible depression and
a terrible war is not served by the same values that satisfied
its parents."[2]

The truth is probably not as dramatic as critics on either
side would have us believe, and in any case we cannot be
too certain. Such authors as Eudora Welty, Peter Taylor,
J. F. Powers, Jean Stafford, Walter Van Tilburg Clark, Jessamyn West, Irwin Shaw, Carson McCullers, Paul Bowles,
Delmore Schwartz, Truman Capote, and Wallace Stegner
are in mid-career. The most the critic can do is examine
their achievements to date, contrast and compare them with
work that has gone before.

A few facts are obvious. In the first place, Southern writers continue their dominance into the 1940's. Eudora Welty,
Peter Taylor, Carson McCullers, and Truman Capote are
all natives of the South; and, following the lead of William
Faulkner, Katherine Anne Porter, Caroline Gordon, and
Robert Penn Warren, take full advantage of the wealth of
material available in the background of their region. The
use of such material, however, is a lesson which has not been
lost upon writers from other areas. Walter Van Tilburg
Clark and Wallace Stegner, for instance, have made use of
the short-story form to examine their own backgrounds in
the Rocky Mountain area in a manner nearer to William
Faulkner than to the agrarian regionalists of the 1920's.

[2] Introduction to *The Best American Short Stories of 1951* (Boston,
Houghton, 1951).

Irwin Shaw's subject matter is divided almost equally between World War II and his urban New York background, with his best stories coming from the latter source. Jessamyn West and J. F. Powers have utilized the religious background of the Quakers and the Roman Catholics in their stories, social groups which have obviously had an immediate and vital influence upon their own lives. Paul Bowles, who is something of a special case, has nevertheless confined his subject matter to the many out-of-the-way places which he has known as an expatriate and world traveler.

In general, we can say, too, that the attitudes of these writers toward their craft is admirable. They appear to view the short-story form not as a means of gaining a livelihood or of building a reputation but as a means whereby significant human values may be disclosed and examined. Their total work is also distinguished by a high percentage of significant stories—stories which, when viewed as the production of a decade, represent an important contribution to the short story in our generation. Such individual works as Eudora Welty's "Powerhouse" and "Old Mr. Marblehall," J. F. Powers's "Lions, Harts, and Leaping Does," Peter Taylor's "A Long Fourth," Irwin Shaw's "The Eighty-Yard Run," and Walter Van Tilburg Clark's "The Wind and the Snow of Winter" form an impressive group of contemporary short stories. As craftsmen, these five authors may be said to have incorporated in their best work most of the virtues of their predecessors of the 1920's and the 1930's. In a sense, and despite their differences, they may be said to be carrying on in the tradition of those authors whose achievements we rate highest in the history of the American short story.

This is the bright side of the picture in the 1940's. That there is another side becomes obvious when we examine the career of each author separately. The first grounds for concern have to do with the low total output and the apparent inability of the best writers of this generation to develop in a manner commensurate with their initial promise. Eudora Welty, for instance, whose career by 1949 (when she published her last volume) seemed most nearly the equal of the careers fashioned during the twenties and thirties, produced her most interesting and competent work in her first volume *A Curtain of Green* published in 1941. This collection of seventeen short stories contained such excellent works as "Lily Daw and the Three Ladies," "A Piece of News," "Petrified Man," "Why I Live at the P.O.," "Clytie," "Old Mr. Marblehall," "Death of a Travelling Salesman," "Powerhouse," and "A Worn Path." Her second volume *The Robber Bridegroom* (1942) was a long story, an experiment in the use of native American legend, which was interesting but which failed primarily because of its confused intentions, its unresolved mixture of broad frontier humor with a too tenuous, perhaps a too feminine, atmosphere of fantasy and dream. The boldness of the concept of this second work was heartening; its failure seemed more to be expected than not—the usual pattern in the development of a new talent. The third collection of stories, published the next year as *The Wide Net, and Other Stories*, followed even more closely the expected pattern. While the total number of outstanding stories was not as great as in the first volume, two were among Miss Welty's best: the title story "The Wide Net" and "Livvie is Back," which won the O. Henry Memorial Award first prize for 1943. After this book appeared, however, three years were to pass before another was published; and *Delta Wedding* (1946), a short novel, had less the characteristics of the novel than it had the appearance of a short story which had been worried into novel length. Here was the first serious break in the continuity of a promising literary career. Then followed another three-year wait and the publication of *The Golden Apples* in 1949. Miss Welty's most recent work is composed of a group of related long stories, each testifying to its author's ability at character delineation and the portrayal of life in a small Southern community, but succeeding neither in its individual section nor in its larger outline to equal in quality the work of her first two collections.

It would be unfair to attempt any general conclusions in regard to Miss Welty's career at this time, even in the light of this apparent falling off both of the quality and the quantity of her writing. After all, five books in less than ten years represents a total not to be taken lightly. It is possible, too, that the reduced tempo of her work represents a gathering of forces, the initiation of a new, more vital, and more completely original period in her work. We must not forget that Miss Welty has undoubtedly established herself as the outstanding writer of her generation. What is alarming about her career is that those characteristics which are the most disturbing—the sudden burst of energy and talent, followed by a reduced productivity—are qualities shared by the most talented of her contemporaries.

The works of Peter Taylor, J. F. Powers, and Walter Van Tilburg Clark have followed a pattern less complete but not unlike that of Miss Welty's. Mr. Powers's fine collection of short stories *The Prince of Darkness and Other Stories* (1947) has been followed by the publication of a few scattered stories in periodicals but not nearly enough to form a second volume. Peter Taylor's *A Long Fourth and Other Stories* (1948) presented seven short stories which had appeared in magazines over a seven-year period, a collection which prompted Robert Penn Warren to state in introducing him: "The stories of *A Long Fourth* are by a very young man. To recur to this fact is not to apologize for the performance here. Instead, it is to congratulate ourselves that we can look forward to many more stories from Peter Taylor. In the fullness of time he will write many more stories, stories probably deeper, fuller, richer, and wiser than these. But it is not probable that those unwritten stories will be any truer than these." Peter Taylor has continued to publish short stories in magazines, particularly in *The New Yorker*, but up to the present his only continued book publication has been a well-constructed but slight novel *A Woman of Means* (1950).

The career which seems most nearly to parallel Miss Welty's is that of Walter Van Tilburg Clark, whose first work was an impressive short novel *The Ox-Bow Incident* (1940), which in its structure and intensity resembled the short-story form almost more than it did the novel. Neither *The City of Trembling Leaves* (1945) nor *The Track of the Cat* (1949) equaled his first attempt, though each was in its own way extremely interesting. A collection of short stories *The Watchful Gods and Other Stories* (1950) was written over a ten-year period, and this book reflects Mr. Clark's continuing efforts to master both his subject matter and his craft. We might point out, as Robie Macauley did in a review of *The Watchful Gods*,[3] that it is just this continuous concern which seems to mark Mr. Clark, more than most others of his generation, as a still developing, still promising writer of fiction in the 1940's. Yet it must not be overlooked, either, that in the ten years during which his writing has appeared, Mr. Clark has not again reached the level of achievement represented by his first work. In this respect, at least, he is characteristic of his generation.

[3] *Furioso* (Winter 1951). See also *Western Review* (Autumn 1951).

I have suggested the possibility that another limitation of the short story of the forties might be an unwillingness on the part of our younger writers to break through the established forms, to find their own subject matter, their own voice, and their own special techniques. In the case of Eudora Welty, J. F. Powers, Peter Taylor, and Walter Van Tilburg Clark, this limitation might be said to reside in the fact that their best stories seem rather a continuation of the excellences of their predecessors (an attempt to master existing techniques) than it is a rebellion against them. It is almost as though the present generation were overawed by the examples already before it, stimulated but also frustrated by them.

As we have seen in the instance of William Saroyan, however, it is not enough merely to find an original mode of expression. Novelty is valueless unless it succeeds in producing new insights into the complexity of experience and developing new processes for the objectification—the artistic display—of those truths with which all important literature provides us. By this I do not mean self-conscious *avant-gardism* but rather the often subtle differences which separate and lend individuality to all great writers or to all important periods—the subtle manner in which Melville differs from Hawthorne, for instance, or Henry James from either of them.

The decade of the forties was not without attempts at such experimentation, the most important of which is probably represented in the short stories of Truman Capote, *A Tree of Night and Other Stories* (1949), or of Paul Bowles, *The Delicate Prey and Other Stories* (1950). Mr. Capote, who was only twenty-four when his first novel *Other Voices, Other Rooms* was published in 1948, has pushed the modern techniques of overt symbolism and atmospheric distortion to an extreme beyond that of any of his contemporaries. With a talent sensitive to the esoteric and the grotesque in human character, his works display a boldness approaching the paintings of the surrealists or the short stories of Franz Kafka. His use of symbols and atmosphere, however, appears finally closer to the methods of Edgar Allan Poe than to the accuracy of specification of either Kafka or William Faulkner—more the presentation of symbols and atmosphere for their own sakes than for the purposes of examination and discovery. The work of Paul Bowles, too, has been likened to that of Poe. His stories are set in out-of-the-way places and filled with events of violence and cruelty, but a violence and cruelty which, because of their very strangeness, seem less horrible to the Western mind than they do merely esoteric—perhaps even romantic. Both of these authors appear to be writing from their own experience—Mr. Capote as a Southerner, Mr. Bowles as an expatriate and traveler; but neither the South of Truman Capote nor the North Africa of Paul Bowles is likely to be taken by the reader for reality in the sense that the South of Eudora Welty and Peter Taylor is—even in the sense that an animal story by Walter Van Tilburg Clark would be. It represents a romantic distortion in which the strangeness is utilized for its own sake—a romantic symbolism in which the symbols, finally, yield little more than their own uniqueness. It represents, in short, only the most modern form of sentimentality, more sophisticated than the sentimentality of a Sherwood Anderson, but lacking also the rugged honesty and the genuine cantankerousness of Anderson.

From Capote and Bowles as a kind of center, a few other writers of the forties seem to range in two directions: in the direction of the symbol for its own sake, as in the case of Shirley Jackson—a brittle and abstract, but "rigged," symbolism; or toward the pure, Anderson-like sentimentality of Frank Brookhouser. Better than these, and in some respects superior to Capote and Bowles, is Robert Lowry, whose volume of short stories *The Wolf that Fed Us* (1947) combines the sentimentality of Anderson with the toughness of Hemingway or of Anderson at his best.

It seems unlikely, however, that the American short story will move either toward the sentimentality of scene and symbol, as in Poe, or toward the simple sentimentality of character portrayal, as in Anderson. Sentimentality represents a trap for the young writer of any age, and what makes Truman Capote and Paul Bowles of particular interest to us here is the possibility that their stories reflect a deep, and perhaps healthy, dissatisfaction with the "well-made" short story of our time, that they may presage a more genuine and a more forceful revolt to follow, if not in their own works, at least in succeeding generations.

ii

Before discussing this possibility, however, let us consider the final hurdle confronting the young writer of the forties, which leads us to a consideration of the conditions under which short stories are published. Almost from the beginning of the century the pages of large-circulation magazines have been closed to writers of originality and talent, at least until that time when the writer has developed a reputation, and with it an audience, through publication elsewhere. What this means is that the young writer has been forced to seek, if not actually to create, his own medium of publication. This he did through the establishment of the so-called "little magazines." Naturally, such publications reflected the particular bias of their contributors so that, like the authors themselves, they divide themselves into two types. First were the political and regional periodicals which flourished primarily in the 1920's and 1930's—*The Masses,* founded in 1911, suppressed during the first war and revived later as *New Masses; Reedy's Mirror* in St. Louis; *The Midland* in Iowa; *The Frontier* in Montana. The second type, for the most part, began by representing the exiles both of Europe and of Greenwich Village, but they were only a little less dispersed than were the organs of social protest. They might be said to have begun with Wyndham Lewis's and Ezra Pound's *Blast* (published in London), continuing through *The Dial* (New York), *The Little Review* (which led a migratory existence), *Poetry* (Chicago), *The Criterion* (London), *transition* (Paris), *Story* (which began in Austria and Spain and moved to New York), and *The Southern Review* (Baton Rouge). The interests of both groups seemed to merge briefly during the period of intense social and political concern of the depression years, but the only influential survivor of this merger today would seem to be the *Partisan Review,* and even here the political interests and aims have been modified considerably since the turbulent years preceding World War II. Just as the major strain in the short story has followed the authors who contributed to the second group of periodicals, rather than the political- and social-minded contributors of the first group, so the periodicals which have flourished during the 1940's—the more conservative, so-called "literary quarterlies"—seem more nearly the descendants of *The Little Review* and *The Southern Review* than they do of even so comparatively eclectic periodicals as *The Midland* and *The Frontier.* In fact, *The Southern Review* would seem to have been the immediate model for

The Kenyon Review, for the more recent years of *The Sewanee Review,* and for *The Hudson Review;* its aims were not too dissimilar from those of such publications as *Accent, Quarterly Review of Literature,* and *The Western Review.*

Of principal interest to us here is the fact that such periodicals did provide opportunities for publication of serious short stories during years when the popular, and even the pseudo-intellectual, magazines were more receptive to popular escape writing and the formula adventure story than they were to works by serious writers. Even today one is not surprised to see such magazines as *The Sewanee Review, The Kenyon Review,* or *Partisan Review* publishing the works of William Faulkner, Katherine Anne Porter, Robert Penn Warren, and Eudora Welty. It is taken for granted by most talented, young, unknown writers that such periodicals are probably their only hope for publication, a fact which was discovered and emphasized by Edward J. O'Brien during the years before his death in 1941 when he was editing his annual *The Best American Short Stories* and which has been stated equally emphatically by his successor, Martha Foley, and by Herschel Brickell, editor of the O. Henry Memorial prize short stories.

Two facts, however, should be stressed, for they have a good deal to do with the health of the short story as a form in the 1940's, and they may shed some light upon the problems which the contemporary writer faces. The first is that although the best and most promising authors of the present time are appearing in the literary quarterlies, these magazines offer far less space for the publication of fiction than they do for the printing of critical essays. The second is that at least a few of the large-circulation periodicals have, during the 1940's, also printed a high proportion of the first-rate short fiction which has appeared.

The relationship of the writer to the literary quarterlies is more complex, and possibly more significant, than it would at first appear. His association with the large-circulation magazines, on the other hand, has been relatively simple since the rebellion of the 1920's when such authors as Sherwood Anderson and Theodore Dreiser convinced themselves that there was no means of compromise between their aims and the editorial requirements of such magazines. With only a few exceptions, authors of the thirties and forties have been printed in the popular magazines on their own terms only—which means, rarely. They have appeared only when the editor was convinced that either the story or the author's reputation would have a wide, immediate appeal. That this appeal was seldom a literary one goes without saying. Even the women's fashion magazines, which have printed more and more excellent short stories, seem to have done so primarily as a means of creating the fashionable atmosphere necessary to their display of ladies' styles. Authors, to be stylish, therefore, must always have achieved a certain popularity, usually through book publication, or their stories should be outstanding examples of what the editor considers the prevailing mode in modern fiction. Nevertheless, these magazines have, over the past decade, provided publication for a remarkable number of high quality short stories. In cases where the editor was a person of taste and distinction, as was true of George Davis, who edited first *Harper's Bazaar* and later *Mademoiselle,* the magazine seemed almost at times to be attempting to establish the mode—that is, to recognize and to accept genuine literary talent, even in beginning and unknown authors.

Such magazines, however, did little to mold, or even influence, the form of the modern short story. They were as incapable of doing it damage as they were of furthering its development. This is less true of another type of mass-appeal periodical, *The New Yorker,* which in the past ten years has developed a kind of short story singular enough to have earned a name of its own: "the *New Yorker* story." The difficulty here is that *The New Yorker's* editorial policy, although it has been as rigid in many ways as the policy of such popular magazines as *The Saturday Evening Post* or *Collier's,* has shown itself perfectly capable of producing—at least of harboring—excellent short stories. As with all editorial rigidity, however, it has tended to produce formula stories—brief, incisive anecdotes, fundamentally a renewal of the local-color story. Its subject matter is that of twentieth-century urban and suburban culture or the romance of far places. Its tone is reportorial and cynical. Its appeal is, in many ways, as snobbish as that of the fashion magazines; but whereas that of the fashion magazines is slanted toward the modern woman's desire to keep up with her neighbor in literature as well as in the latest dress modes, the appeal of *The New Yorker* short story is to those readers whom Peter Viereck has designated "the new-style Babbitts": pseudo intellectuals, whose pretensions are perhaps an apotheosis of the hardness and the cynicism of the 1920's.

What is important to us here, however, is not the reading public which *The New Yorker* has engendered but the number of talented young writers which it has attracted. Such authors as Irwin Shaw, Mark Schorer, Paul Bowles, Edward Newhouse, J. D. Salinger, and Peter Taylor are regular contributors. Many of them are paid a kind of professional retaining fee by which they obligate themselves to submit all of their work to that magazine. Many are obliged, we can assume, to submit to the notorious *New Yorker* blue pencil, by which, as one of the above authors said publicly a short while ago, even the most apparently different kind of short story can be turned at once into a *New Yorker* story. Such a policy, while it avoids the obviously sentimental and inconsequential level of much popular fiction, does result in standardization—a general level of mediocrity, which fact may have something to do with the failure of authors such as Irwin Shaw, Mark Schorer, and Edward Newhouse to fulfill the promise of their earlier work.

Charges similar to these have been made against the literary quarterlies, so that it is not uncommon to hear stories referred to as typical *Kenyon Review* or typical *Partisan Review* short stories. If such charges are true, they are probably more true of these two publications than of the general run of the smaller magazines. Certainly the literary excellence of both *Kenyon Review* and *Partisan Review* depends less upon the quality of their fiction than it does upon their editorial discrimination in the publication of criticism and poetry. One is more likely to find genuinely important fiction in the pages of *The Sewanee Review, Accent, Furioso, Epoch* or, *The Western Review*, short stories by such authors as William Faulkner, Robert Penn Warren, Caroline Gordon, Katherine Anne Porter, Eudora Welty, Walter Van Tilburg Clark, J. F. Powers, and Robert Lowry among those authors already mentioned; but particularly one is more likely to find here the first publication of those authors whose work will only become better known in the second half of the century. Even so, and despite the fact that the *Partisan Review* and *Kenyon Review* short stories do tend to run into a somewhat consistent pattern, these magazines have introduced the work of such authors as Lionel Trilling, Delmore Schwartz, Saul Bellow, John Berryman, Mary McCarthy, and Arthur Mizener. Despite their relatively low circulation (few of these magazines print more than three thousand copies per issue) and their relatively

low rates of payment, however, the literary quarterlies—
and their predecessors, the little magazines—have furnished
initial publication for a great majority of the important
short-story writers of our century; so that it seems clear
that their chief limitation at the present time is not their
editorial rigidity but rather—a fact which has already been
mentioned—their predominantly critical interests, a condition which relegates the publication of fiction to at least
a secondary role, even among those periodicals which have
done, and are still doing, the most in the development of
the American short story in our century.

This interest of the literary quarterlies in the problems
of criticism should not surprise us when we consider that
these periodicals have been at the forefront of a critical
movement known as "The New Criticism," which came
to a kind of fruition in the 1940's. Its development has been
suggested in Chapter 1. Its relationship to many of the authors under consideration in this chapter is not yet entirely
clear. The effects of this interest have been more directly
felt in the classrooms of the universities and in the pages of
the serious magazines than by the writers of short stories
themselves. There is little question, however, that modern
American writing in all fields has been profoundly affected
by the quality and the intensity of American criticism since
the end of World War I. In the first place, our serious authors have written in an atmosphere dominated by critical
ideas. Whether they have rebelled against or accepted the
attitudes of the New Criticism, few have remained unaware
of them. If it is true that many of the readers of the quarterlies are writers, as is certainly true, then the very interest
shown in critical discussion—even at the expense of fiction
and verse—is at least partly the result of an increased interest on the part of the writers themselves. Also, the very fact

of an increased consciousness of aesthetic problems by the American short-story writer would seem to be evidence enough that he has not been unaffected by the critical temper of his times.

What is this temper, and how is it particularly related to the generation of the 1940's? In answering such questions we move perhaps further than is justifiable from the level of discussion and into the realm of speculation. We have suggested that the predominant interest of the literary magazines has been in criticism; also, we have suggested that the authors of short stories, as contributors and readers, have not themselves been entirely disinterested. But it is not in the magazines alone—and perhaps not even primarily in the magazines—that the critical attitude has been most effective. On a very practical level, the New Criticism was a revolt against the manner in which literature was being taught in the universities—a rebellion against dry-as-dust scholarship which the American educational system had inherited from nineteenth-century European universities as well as against literary impressionism which was our inheritance from the genteel tradition at the turn of the century. The period from 1930 to 1940 may be described as a decade when critical reforms first made themselves felt on the campuses of American universities. Such a fact would be of little importance here if it had not also marked the time when many American writers, including perhaps the best of our contemporary short-story writers, were also to be found upon university campuses. Robert Penn Warren, Caroline Gordon, Lionel Trilling, Peter Taylor, J. F. Powers, Walter Van Tilburg Clark, Delmore Schwartz, Mark Schorer, Jessamyn West, Saul Bellow, Arthur Mizener, and Wallace Stegner have all been, or still are, connected with university English departments. Regular instruction in the craft of fiction-writing is available at the present time in most American universities.

Whether it was a critical interest in the problems of literature which led to such a development or whether both were no more than a reflection of a need on the part of writers and teachers to revitalize their professions need not concern us here. Of first importance is the fact that the decade of the 1940's experienced such a development, with the obvious result that American writing in all forms has been both stimulated and altered by it. How far, and in exactly what ways, it has been altered, it is too early to say. What does seem clear, however, is that American writers as a group, and outside of all regional boundaries, have developed a searching and serious attitude toward their craft for the first time in the history of our literature.

One way to look at such a phenomenon is to see it as only a broader, more communal, interest in problems with which our major artists have been concerned from the beginning. If the attitudes developed during this period persist—as they are likely to do—they may even result in diminishing the sense of isolation and uncertainty under which such writers as Hawthorne, Melville, Emily Dickinson, and Mark Twain labored in the past; they may come to represent an answer to the charges that America's terrain is too vast, her regional temperaments too various, to produce any single and integrated attitude toward literature. With the American state university serving as patron of the arts, perhaps we may have discovered a satisfactory compromise between the political dangers of official government sponsorship and the uncertainties of private support.

The advantages and disadvantages of such a situation concern us only insofar as they appear to affect the writers of the present generation. The dangers, as they have been

pointed out by those opposed to such a trend, would seem
to consist in a tendency toward conservatism, toward a general level—even if a very high one—of "sameness"; toward
the establishment of coteries and groups with serious, but
similar, attitudes and intentions; toward a development of
technical facility at the expense of native insight and originality. It is such thinking which leads to the conclusions
already mentioned—that our young writers have learned
too much too fast. Malcolm Cowley has said that young
writers today are too intent upon gaining economic security
—that they lack the spirit which moved their predecessors
of the 1920's to take chances—"to go out on a limb." Stephen
Spender, the British poet, has said of young American writers that they are too concerned with the problems of form
—problems which a European takes for granted.

Certainly it is true that the ideal creative condition results when the artist has completely assimilated his technical knowledge, when the act of writing has become almost
completely unconscious, yet still conditioned by a knowledge which has become a part of the writer himself. It is a
recognized fact that the ability of the writer to concentrate
upon his subject represents a sign of his creativity. As T. S.
Eliot has suggested, the moment of creation is no time for
the artist to educate himself—to shape himself as a creative being. Conscious concern with literary principles can
come only before and after the primary act of composition.
Such knowledge will prove inhibiting until the writer has
learned to apply it as naturally as the painter applies his
knowledge of color, rhythm, and design, or as the musician,
his knowledge both of musical theory and of the instru-
ment upon which he performs.

The traditional fault of American writing has always
seemed to be a lack of concern for the elementary tech-

niques of the craft. As we have seen, this represents the great limitation of writers in the naturalist tradition. Such knowledge, as Mr. Spender suggests, artists in other lands have not lacked, but the best of them have possessed it as a part of their national tradition. Having once possessed it, they are then free to rebel against it, to explode the old forms, and to strive toward the creation of a new synthesis, which is the unending struggle and impossible condition of the highest forms of art.

It is in this sense that the artist is a revolutionary, a rebel, and an experimentalist. Not that he lacks respect for form, but that he takes relatively little satisfaction from forms already achieved. The nature of great literature is paradoxical, as is all truth. To paraphrase the Christian injunction, we might say that the artist, in order to achieve form, must first destroy it. And confusing as this seems at times to the ordinary reader, it is the mark of such great works of fiction as *Tom Jones, Tristram Shandy, War and Peace, The Brothers Karamazov, Madame Bovary, Moby Dick*, and *Ulysses* that they introduced unfamiliar elements, applied new techniques, and thus altered the old forms. In the short story it is equally true of the works of Chekhov, Henry James, James Joyce, Franz Kafka, and William Faulkner.

Despite the achievements of individual American writers, it is not yet certain that our writers as a whole have learned this lesson. Herman Melville learned it at the expense of an alienated reading public, and there are indications that he died insecure in his knowledge. William Faulkner has made a point of denying a knowledge of that art which is perfectly obvious in the best of his work. If writers of the forties, therefore, seem too consciously and too exclusively preoccupied with such problems, such preoccupation at least eliminates the dangers of hasty and inconsequential work. As a fault, it is the opposite of the careless, intuitive attitude which we have come to think of as typically American. I should like to suggest the possibility that it is only a temporary and necessary stage in a transition from awkward and self-conscious literary apprenticeship to a new concept of responsibility and knowledge, which may come to represent the maturing of American creative talent. Even in life such a transition is difficult, and there will always be regrets for the loss of youthful innocence and vitality. However, we do not therefore conclude that maturity is nothing but the first signs of decay. Early maturity may be marked by an attitude of too great conservatism after the incontinences of youth, but this is not decadence. It is rather the gathering together of energies heretofore too little considered, too little utilized, and without which complete development is impossible.

In terms of the American short story, such may well be the case. Complete maturity may or may not be achieved by the present generation. Yet it seems likely now that we may someday come to view the short story as the particular form through which American letters finally came of age, through which the life of its people and the vision of its artists most nearly approached full expression.

A SELECTED BIBLIOGRAPHY

A Selected Bibliography

I. BIBLIOGRAPHIES

Because no essays are indexed here, such standard bibliographical references as *The International Index* and *The Readers' Guide* are cited. Additional books of and on the short story are listed in *Books in Print* and in earlier titles in that series. The most useful subject headings in these volumes are "American Fiction," "American Literature," "Fiction," and "Short Stories." Additional periodicals are referred to in the Colegrove volume listed below. The Hoffman volume contains a Bibliography of almost all the books on prose fiction in general and on the novel in particular which will be of value to the reader and student of the short story.

Aldridge, John (ed.). (See Section III below.)

Charles, Dorothy, and Doris Dart (eds.). *International Index to Periodicals.* New York, H. W. Wilson Co., annual publication.

Colegrove, Harriett, *et al. Index to Little Magazines.* Denver, Alan Swallow, Publisher, annual publication.

Cook, Dorothy E., and Isabel S. Monro. *Fiction Catalogue, 1941 Edition.* New York, H. W. Wilson Co., 1942. (Subsequent editions, edited by Miss Cook and Estelle A. Fidell, became available in 1947, 1949, 1950, 1951.)

Crawford, Bartholow V., Alexander C. Kern, and Morriss H. Needleman. *An Outline History of American Literature.* New York, Barnes and Noble, Inc., 1945.

Firkins, Ina Ten Eyck. *Index to Short Stories.* Second and enlarged edition. New York, H. W. Wilson Co., 1923. (A supplement was published in 1929, a second one in 1936.)

Foley, Martha. (See Section II below.)

Grossman, Regina Goldman, and Nina R. Thompson (eds.). *The Cumulative Book Index.* New York, H. W. Wilson Co., annual publication.

Hoffman, Frederick J. *The Modern Novel in America, 1900-1950.* Chicago, Henry Regnery Co., 1951. (See note above.)

Millett, Fred B. *Contemporary American Authors.* Revised edition. New York, Harcourt, Brace and Company, 1940.

Robinson, Sarita, Bertha Joel, and Mary Keyes. *The Readers' Guide to Periodical Literature.* New York, H. W. Wilson Co., annual publication.

Spiller, Robert E., *et al. A Literary History of the United States.* Volume III. New York, The Macmillan Company, 1949.

Trent, William Peterfield, *et al. Cambridge History of American Literature.* New York, G. P. Putnam's Sons, 1917-21.

West, Ray B., Jr. *Essays in Modern Literary Criticism, an Anthology.* New York, Rinehart and Co., 1952.

Zabel, D. Morton. *Literary Opinion in America.* Revised edition. New York, Harper and Brothers, Publishers, 1951.

II. ANTHOLOGIES

The anthologies listed below have been included because they contain critical material on the stories they offer, or they present experimental material or other trends in short fiction, or they present the works of those authors whose works are often difficult to obtain elsewhere. Anthologies which deal with authors of the twenties or earlier are too plentiful to include.

Brickell, Herschel (ed.). *Prize Stories of . . . , The O. Henry Awards*. Garden City, N. Y., Doubleday and Company, Inc., annual publication.

Brooks, Cleanth, Jr., and Robert Penn Warren (eds.). *Understanding Fiction*. New York, F. S. Crofts, 1943.

Cross, E. A. (ed.). *Book of the Short Story*. Selected and edited with the history and technique of the short story. New York, American Book Company, 1934.

Current-Garcia, Eugene, and Walton R. Patrick (eds.). *American Short Stories: 1820 to the Present*. Chicago, Scott, Foresman and Company, 1952.

Fifty-Five Short Stories from The New Yorker. New York, Simon and Schuster, Inc., 1949.

Foley, Martha (ed.). *The Best American Short Stories*. Boston, Houghton Mifflin Co., annual publication.

——, and A. A. Rothberg (eds.). *U. S. Stories; Regional Stories from the Forty-eight States*. New York, Hendricks House, 1949.

Gilkes, Lillian, and Warren Bower (eds.). *Short Story Craft*. New York, The Macmillan Company, 1949.

Gordon, Caroline, and Allen Tate (eds.). *The House of Fiction: An Anthology of the Short Story with Commentary.* New York, Charles Scribner's Sons, 1950.

Hathaway, Baxter (ed.). *Writers for Tomorrow; A Collection of Fiction by Writers of Tomorrow for Readers of Today.* Ithaca, N. Y., Cornell University Press, 1948.

Heilman, Robert B. (ed.). *Modern Short Stories.* New York, Harcourt, Brace and Company, 1950.

Kielty, Bernardine (ed.). *Treasury of Short Stories.* New York, Simon and Schuster, Inc., 1947.

Laughlin, James (ed.). *New Directions.* Norfolk, Conn., and New York, New Directions, annual publication.

O'Brien, Edward J. (ed.). *Short Story Case Book.* New York, Farrar and Rinehart, Inc., 1935.

Schorer, Mark (ed.). *The Story: A Critical Anthology.* New York, Prentice-Hall, Inc., 1950.

Stegner, Wallace, and Richard Snowcroft (eds.). *Stanford Short Stories.* Stanford, Calif., Stanford University Press, 1946, 1948, 1949, 1950, 1951.

———, and Boris Ilyin. *The Writer's Art: A Collection of Short Stories.* Boston, D. C. Heath and Company, 1950.

Tate, Allen, and John Peale Bishop (eds.). *American Harvest.* New York, L. B. Fischer Publishing Corp., 1942.

Warren, Robert Penn (ed.). *A Southern Harvest; Short Stories by Southern Writers.* Boston, Houghton, Mifflin Co., 1937.

West, Ray B., Jr., and Robert W. Stallman. *The Art of Modern Fiction.* New York, Rinehart and Co., Inc., 1949.

A number of magazines have regularly printed stories of considerable interest. These include: *Accent, American Prefaces* (1935-43), *The Atlantic Monthly, Epoch, Furioso, Harper's Bazaar, Harper's Magazine, The Hopkins Review, The Hudson*

Review, The Kenyon Review, Mademoiselle, The New Yorker, The Pacific Spectator, Partisan Review, The Sewanee Review, The Southern Review (1935–42), *Tomorrow* (1941–51), *The University of Kansas City Review, The Western Review* (formerly *The Rocky Mountain Review*).

III. CRITICISM AND HISTORY
OF THE SHORT STORY

For essays, the reader is referred to Section I above. For books on the novel but of considerable value to the reader and student of the short story, the reader is referred to the Hoffman volume in Section I above. The traditionally accepted books on the short story written early in this century and of ever-decreasing value and now mainly of historical interest, as well as textbooks for fiction-writing courses, have been infrequently included below. Bibliographies including them are found in the volumes edited by Blodgett, by Ellis, and by Pence, which are listed below for this reason.

Aldridge, John (ed.). *Critiques and Essays on Modern Fiction.* With a Foreword by Mark Schorer and Bibliography by Robert W. Stallman. New York, Ronald Press Company, 1952.

Baker, H. T. *The Contemporary Short Story.* Boston, D. C. Heath and Company, 1916.

Bement, Douglas. *Weaving the Short Story.* New York, Richard R. Smith Publisher, Inc., 1931.

Blodgett, Harold (ed.). *Short Story Survey.* Chicago, New York, Philadelphia, J. B. Lippincott Co., 1939.

Brooks, Cleanth, Jr., and Robert Penn Warren. (See Section II above.)

Ellis, Amanda M. (ed.). *Representative Short-Stories.* New York, Thomas Nelson and Sons, 1932.

Gordon, Caroline, and Allen Tate. (See Section II above.)

Grabo, Carl H. *The Art of the Short Story.* New York, Charles Scribner's Sons, 1913.

Howells, William Dean. *Criticism and Fiction.* New York, Harper and Brothers, Publishers, 1892.

James, Henry. *The Art of the Novel: Critical Prefaces.* Edited and with an Introduction by Richard P. Blackmur. New York, Charles Scribner's Sons, 1934.

――――. *The Art of Fiction and Other Essays.* With an Introduction by Morris Roberts. New York, Oxford Univ. Press, 1948.

Matthews, Brander. *The Philosophy of the Short-Story.* New York, Longmans, Green and Co., Inc., 1901. (Written 1884.)

O'Brien, Edward J. *The Advance of the Short Story.* Revised edition. New York, Dodd, Mead and Company, 1931.

――――. *The Dance of the Machines; The American Short Story and the Industrial Age.* New York, The Macaulay Company, 1929.

――――. (See Section II above.)

O'Connor, William Van (ed.). *Forms of Modern Fiction.* Minneapolis, University of Minnesota Press, 1948.

Pattee, Fred Lewis. *The Development of the American Short Story: An Historical Survey.* New York, Harper and Brothers, Publishers, 1923.

Pence, Raymond Woodbury (ed.). *Short Stories by Present Day Authors.* New York, The Macmillan Company, 1922.

Schorer, Mark. (See Section II above.)

Wellek, René, and Austin Warren. *Theory of Literature.* With Notes and Bibliography. New York, Harcourt, Brace and Company, 1949. (See especially "The Nature and Modes of Narrative Fiction.")

Welty, Eudora. *Short Stories.* New York, Harcourt, Brace and Company, 1950. (An earlier, privately distributed edition was entitled *The Reading and Writing of Short Stories.*)

West, Ray B., Jr. (See Section I above.)

——, and Robert W. Stallman. (See Section II above.)

Wharton, Edith. *The Writing of Fiction.* New York, Charles Scribner's Sons, 1925.

Zabel, D. Morton. (See Section I above.)

INDEX

INDEX

Page numbers set in *italics* indicate the major critical reference.